This unauthorized history of *Star Trek* is the complete and inspirational chronicle of a legend from its original conception to its phenomenal effect on millions of viewers across the world. America's leading science fiction television historian James Van Hise takes you where no *Trek* fan has ever gone before—from the meeting in which Gene Roddenberry first pitched his idea for the *Star Trek* series to the lean years when die-hard fans kept the show alive to the continuing sequence of successful feature films and new television series which have secured *Star Trek*'s enduring importance in popular culture, and in our lives. The origins of the series are revealed through in-depth interviews with the original cast and creative staff, offering not only a wealth of *Trek* trivia but speculations as to what the future may hold.

Here are the facts behind the science fiction, the historical journey that goes beyond what you can see on the screen and covers three decades of voyage and on-going discover.

Look for

TREK: THE UNAUTHORIZED A-Z
by Hal Schuster and Wendy Rathbone

**THE UNAUTHORIZED TREKKERS'
GUIDE TO THE NEXT GENERATION
AND DEEP SPACE NINE**
by James Van Hise

**SCI-FI TV: FROM THE TWILIGHT ZONE TO
DEEP SPACE NINE**
by James Van Hise

STAR TREK MEMORIES
by William Shatner with Chris Kreski

STAR TREK MOVIE MEMORIES
by William Shatner with Chris Kreski

Published by HarperPrism

THE UNAUTHORIZED
HISTORY OF
TREK

JAMES VAN HISE

HarperPrism
An Imprint of HarperPaperbacks

HarperPaperbacks   *A Division of* HarperCollins*Publishers*
10 East 53rd Street, New York, N.Y. 10022

A trade paperback edition of this book was published in 1991 by Pioneer Books, Inc.

Cover photograph by Rob Atkins/The Image Bank

First HarperPaperbacks printing: November 1995

Printed in the United States of America

HarperPrism is an imprint of HarperPaperbacks. HarperPaperbacks, HarperPrism, and colophon are trademarks of HarperCollins*Publishers*

❖ 10 9 8 7 6 5 4 3 2 1

CONTENTS

FOREWORD

GENE RODDENBERRY (1921–1991)

It came as a surprise to many when Gene Roddenberry died of a heart attack on October 24, 1991. While the news that he had suffered a series of strokes during the year had leaked out, the full extent of his illness was not known.

There had been rumors, though, when a gala twenty-fifth anniversary celebration for *Star Trek* at Paramount was scaled down in September because he was too ill to attend. A couple of actors from the original series had long been rumored to be in frail health, but no one ever thought Roddenberry would be the first to depart.

While some fear that with Roddenberry's passing the light of *Star Trek* will die, it has been known for some time that he was all but retired, having stepped down from his on-line duties on *The Next Generation* more and more as each year passed, until for the last two years he had been little more than a consultant. His involvement with the motion pictures has been minimal since the first one, the only one on which he worked full-time.

Star Trek was a synthesis of many talents. While it was created by Roddenberry years ago, it was developed by such people as Gene Coon, Dorothy Fontana, and others whose contributions added much to the legend. While Roddenberry had the original vision and steered the ship on a true course, he was not the only one to dream the dream, and his biggest gift was to inspire others. The many forms of *Star Trek* over the years serve as living testimonial.

When people die there is the danger of their being elevated to a role they never had in life or never aspired to. One should not suddenly elevate Roddenberry to godhood. Gene was a man, with the foibles of a man, but he should never be forgotten for his many abilities, and most of all for his dream, a dream he shared with so many of us. This dream will insure that Gene Roddenberry will never be forgotten.

JAMES VAN HISE

A PHENOMENON UNEXCELLED

tar Trek. These two simple words bring forth a vast web of mental associations to millions of people. For more than twenty-five years, a remarkable and widely varied group of characters has seemingly taken over a sizable portion of our collective consciousness and made it its own. Perhaps the late science fiction visionary Philip K. Dick saw this when he had a character in his novel *A Scanner Darkly* refer to the latest entertainment extravaganza as a "captainkirk."

More than thirty years after Gene Roddenberry first envisioned the world of the starship *Enterprise*, the traces of the original series are everywhere. Kirk and crew have become icons in American popular culture, representing the best of our dreams: adventure, exploration, the triumph of the human spirit over all kinds of adversity. Current films and television series continue to refer to *Star Trek,* and in the 1991 feature film

Bill and Ted's Bogus Journey William Shatner is honored as a guest star when the movie's heroes are seen watching "The Arena."

Clearly, *Star Trek* has risen above the fate of other past television programs. This is a show to which some people have dedicated more than twenty-five years of their lives, often making *Star Trek* a centerpiece of their own personal philosophies and mythologies. This is a show that has refused to die. Battling network muddleheadedness in the sixties, creator Gene Roddenberry thought that his dream had died after its third season.

Fortunately, nothing could undermine or destroy *Star Trek*'s unique appeal. Rather than fade gracefully away into the dusty attic of quaint and anachronistic conceits, *Star Trek* continued to live and breathe. With only seventy-nine episodes aired, the myth of *Star Trek* built around the dedication of its fans as well as an undying fascination with a television show that had shown viewers such strange new worlds. Even Roddenberry was somewhat taken aback by the support his creation gathered as the years went by; it began to seem inevitable that *Star Trek* would return someday, and overcome the many impediments that blocked its path.

Star Trek brought fortune and fame to a handful of actors who had for years been laboring in obscurity: William Shatner, Leonard Nimoy, DeForest Kelley, Nichelle Nichols, James Doohan, George Takei, and Walter Koenig. Without their talents, this unique television legacy would never have survived. Instead of fading into celluloid, these actors became a surrogate family, a group of faithful and fascinating friends to a generation, and, now, to that generation's children.

Though some found the 1979 release of *Star Trek: The Motion Picture* to be disappointing, the movie's tepid reviews could not slow down the rampaging phenomenon of *Star Trek*'s popularity. Fans remained as involved as ever, and were irate at Spock's death in *The Wrath of Khan* and the destruction of their beloved *Enterprise* in *The Search for Spock*. No amount of irritation or criticism could keep Trekkers out of the movie theaters, however, and hard-core fans began to share seat space with a new generation, born in the time since Kirk's last journey. Disgruntlement among the fans was overcome by loyalty, and eventually passed into the legend of *Star Trek*.

The original *Enterprise* crew had been busy in the intervening years. In 1986, when the fourth, and most successful, movie was released, fans were thrilled to find Leonard Nimoy in the director's chair. The lighthearted approach, combined with a compelling and timely *Enterprise* mission to Earth's history, served to bring yet more new fans into the *Star Trek* fold.

Rumors of a new *Star Trek* incarnation abounded for nearly twenty years, and 1987 finally brought the debut of the *Enterprise* D, a Galaxy-class starship, in *Star Trek: The Next Generation*. Launched on Stardate 2363, some one hundred years after the last voyage of the now legendary Captain Kirk, the new *Enterprise* was a sleek beauty that never forgot her roots in rough-and-ready adventure. Captained by Patrick Stewart as Jean-Luc Picard, the new *Enterprise* would have strong ensemble acting by Jonathan Frakes, Brent Spiner, Gates McFadden, Marina Sirtis, LeVar Burton, Denise Crosby, and Michael Dorn. Like their predecessors on the bridge, the names of this crew rapidly became household words, their characters and actions debated, analyzed, applauded, and criticized.

The launch of the *Enterprise* D set off a raging, still-unresolved debate about which captain and crew best exemplified the dream of *Star Trek*. Fans took sides immediately and began fantasizing about a meeting, and an inevitable fight, between the two captains. If some fans found the new product unpalatable, *Star Trek: The Next Generation* widened the fold, and in its seven-year run garnered its own acclaim, awards, and admirers.

Gene Roddenberry's dream continued to explore strange new worlds, and in 1993, two years after its creator's death, *Star Trek* gave birth to *Star Trek: Deep Space Nine,* a new weekly series set in a permanent orbiting space station. The world of *Trek* met Avery Brooks as Commander Sisko, with actors Rene Auberjonois, Nana Visitor, Terry Farrell, Siddig El Fadil, Armin Shimerman, and Colm Meaney to man the station.

Two more movies, *Star Trek V: The Final Frontier* (1988), and *Star Trek VI: The Undiscovered Country* (1991), kept fans in the theaters, when they weren't home watching Picard in first-run shows and Kirk and Spock in popular reruns.

Star Trek: The Next Generation saw its final broadcast in 1994, but fans had been promised a movie. The autumn release of *Star Trek: Generations* may have been weak critically, but fans were treated to a long-awaited meeting of Picard and Kirk. The long-debated "battle of the captains" did not materialize, as the movie showed the two *Enterprise* captains working together in a spirit of cooperation, not conflict. Like other *Trek* movies, *Generations* itself was born in conflict, and fans missed the presence of Leonard Nimoy and DeForest Kelley.

If Kirk seemed to be passing the torch, although with chagrin, to Picard, *Star Trek: The Next Generation* found its own child in the launch of yet another weekly series. In January 1995, Paramount launched its own broadcast network, UPN, with the maiden voyage of *Star Trek: Voyager.* The starship *Voyager* is thrown nearly eighty million light-years from home, and the new series chronicles the ship's travels as it makes its way back to Federation space. Captain Kathryn Janeway has already been compared to both James T. Kirk and Katharine Hepburn. Actress Kate

Mulgrew and crew, confident and excited, are gearing up for the inevitable scrutiny of *Star Trek*'s legendary fandom.

On inheriting Gene Roddenberry's formidable responsibility and vision, Executive Producer Rick Berman told *TV Guide* in the spring 1995 special edition, "We would be crazy if we always sat around saying to ourselves, 'Now what would Gene have done about this?' I owe him a great deal, and part of that debt is to keep his vision as true as I can—but not so rigidly that *Star Trek* doesn't grow."

All *Star Trek* fans owe Roddenberry a great deal of love and admiration for his creativity, dedication, and integrity. While *Star Trek* began as a concept that few thought would ever get off the ground, the starship *Enterprise* became the flagship of a fleet of wondrous ships and stories that after nearly thirty years continue, almost unbelievably, to boldly go where no one has gone before. This book will take you on that journey, from Roddenberry's first idea to the final frontier.

GUS MEYER

CHAPTER ONE:

A DREAM IN THE MAKING

.

ene Roddenberry was a science fiction aficionado from childhood. It all started with a battered copy of *Astounding* magazine and took off from there. Still, he never considered writing in any genre or medium until much later in life.

In the late forties he worked as an international airline pilot for Pan Am, and it was at this time that he began to write pieces for flying magazines. In 1948, he was one of only eight survivors of a plane crash in the Syrian desert, an experience that profoundly shaped his attitude toward life.

The writing bug soon led him to quit the airline and move to Los Angeles, where he met with absolutely no success in the new field of television writing. The industry was, at the time, still centered on the East Coast. This led him to become a Los Angeles policeman, a job which would provide him with insights no office job could ever hope to offer. At the same time, he continued to write, and sold his first script, pseudonymously, in 1951.

More sales followed, including "The Secret Defense of 117," a science fiction story which aired on *Chevron Theater* and starred Ricardo Montalban. During the same period, he wrote speeches for L.A. police chief William Parker, and even ghosted most of Parker's book *Parker on Police,* still regarded today as a classic of police philosophy.

Roddenberry managed to slip a bit of his own more liberal views into right-wing Parker's texts; Parker was often perplexed when people he regarded as left-wingers would enthusiastically applaud his Roddenberry-penned speeches. Despite Parker's strong political stance, there was a side to him that impressed Roddenberry even more: he was always open to new ideas, and had wide-ranging intellectual interests, traits which Roddenberry would later incorporate into the character of Spock.

By 1954, Roddenberry's moonlighting was earning him four times his policeman's salary, leading him to resign from the force and devote all his energies to writing. After freelancing for a variety of series, including *Dragnet, Naked City,* and *Dr. Kildare,* he became head writer of the Richard Boone Western series, *Have Gun Will Travel.*

He began to realize that freelancing left the final product of his mind in the hands of others. To retain control over his ideas (and to retain greater profits), he decided to become a producer. He had seen too many pilots written but left unmade; it was time for him to see one all the way through to completion.

His first series was thus created: *The Lieutenant,* which ran for the 1963 television season. Starring Gary Lockwood as a newly commissioned officer in the peacetime Marine Corps, this was an intelligent, dramatic series which unfortunately failed to draw much of an audience.

(Ironically, another Marine-centered series which premiered the following year was successful enough to last through the rest of the decade. *Gomer Pyle* was not, however, noted for its intelligence!) One episode featured an actor named Leonard Nimoy as a flamboyant Hollywood director; Roddenberry would eventually employ him again in the new series he was already creating.

By the time *The Lieutenant* went off the air, Roddenberry had submitted a proposed *Star Trek* format to MGM, the studio behind *The Lieutenant*. The basic premise was the one now familiar to millions, but the characters were radically different.

The Captain was one Robert T. April, his executive officer was the logical female Number One, and the navigator was one José Tyler. The doctor was nicknamed Bones but was otherwise an older, completely different character. Mr. Spock was in the proposal, but was described as having "a red-hued satanic look" and, according to one source, absorbed energy through a red plate in his navel!

The *Enterprise* and its mission are perhaps the only things that made it to the screen unchanged from this original format. One other thing Roddenberry insisted on was that the science fiction in the show be ordered and logical, without falling on convenient fantasy resolutions having no basis in reality.

MGM said it was interested, but not at the present time. Other studios followed suit, providing Roddenberry with a fileful of politely worded brush-offs. A shift in the prevailing winds occurred when he learned that Desilu Studios was looking for series ideas. Desilu, the studio behind *I Love Lucy* and Lucille Ball's later shows, was hurting financially; *Lucy* was its only viable property, and it frequently rented out its facilities to other studios to make up for the monthly overhead costs. Desilu was impressed with Roddenberry and his ideas, including the

Star Trek proposal, and signed him to a three-year pilot development deal. (Desilu's interest in *Star Trek* would pass over to Paramount Pictures when Paramount bought the television studio out.) Things seemed to pick up steam almost immediately, as Roddenberry was called in to pitch *Star Trek* to an assembly of CBS's highest-ranking network executives.

They listened for two hours. Roddenberry was convinced that he'd sold them on it. They were certainly interested in his thoughts on saving costs and designing ships, among other things, but their questions turned out to have another motive entirely. When he was finished, they thanked him politely, but passed on the proposal, as they already had a science fiction series of their own in the works. Roddenberry may very well have inadvertently helped them launch *Lost in Space,* which even, by some coincidence, had the Robinson family embarking on a five-year mission of exploration. *Lost in Space* premiered in 1965 and, like *Star Trek,* ran for three seasons.

Roddenberry, even though disheartened by CBS's cavalier treatment of him, kept on trying. In May of 1964, NBC offered Roddenberry twenty thousand dollars in story development money. The deal was that Roddenberry would develop three story ideas for a *Star Trek* pilot, then write a pilot script based on the idea chosen by the network. NBC chose the story entitled "The Cage." Roddenberry set to work on a shooting script. In September of 1964, the script was approved: the first *Star Trek* episode had received the green light.

Roddenberry had already been laying the groundwork for this. Of primary importance was the starship *Enterprise* itself, which he hoped to have avoid all previous spaceship clichés.

The final design of the U.S.S. *Enterprise* was largely the work of assistant art director Matt Jefferies, who had a strong background in aviation.

During World War Two, Jefferies flew B-17 missions over Africa, and later devoted much of his spare time to restoring vintage airplanes. The starship and its various sets were drawn from Jefferies's own familiarity with aeronautics.

As a member of the Aviation Writers' Association, Jefferies was able to collate a large number of designs from NASA and the defense industry . . . all as examples of what *not* to do. All previous science fiction spaceship designs were also held up as things to be avoided.

Hundreds of sketches were made for the design of the *Enterprise*; the main hull was, at one point, going to be spherical, and even the now-familiar final design almost wound up being shot upside down. (Admittedly, this wouldn't make much difference in space.) As a final touch of authenticity, red and green lights were added on the port and starboard sides, a time-honored nautical practice. Finally, a three-foot and fourteen-foot model of the *Enterprise* were constructed.

Again, Matt Jefferies's air force engineering background came in handy in the design of the sets. The U.S. Navy was so impressed by the bridge design that it supposedly used it as a basis for one of its own communications centers.

Another seemingly insurmountable problem revolved around Roddenberry's desire to feature a green-skinned woman in the pilot. For some reason, all the makeup department's experiments failed to show up on the test footage shot of actress Susan Oliver for this purpose. No matter how dark they made the green, their model always showed up on film as looking perfectly normal. Eventually, they discovered that someone at the photo lab, perplexed by the pictures coming his way, was chemically correcting what he thought was a flaw in the initial photography. When this was cleared up, the desired makeup effect was achieved with a minimum of fuss.

"The Cage" began shooting with a cast of characters

drawn from the original format, although the captain was now named Christopher Pike. Pike was portrayed by Jeffrey Hunter, who had the rare distinction of having once played Jesus Christ, in *King of Kings*. John Hoyt played the ship's doctor, Philip Boyce. Leonard Nimoy appeared as Spock, but the character was a bit different from its later incarnation, as the logical aspect of his future personality belonged to the character Number One, portrayed by Majel Barrett.

Leonard Nimoy had assumed that he would be trying out for the part of Spock; he failed to realize that he was Roddenberry's first and preferred choice for the role. The prospect of a regular series was exciting to the actor, who, despite his frequent guest appearances on television, did not have what could be called a stable income. He did have some misgivings about the part; what if the show was an unmitigated flop? Would he become a laughingstock, forever derided for having dared to don those silly-looking pointed ears? In conference with his friend Vic Morrow, he even pondered the possibility of developing character makeup that would completely conceal his true face—just in case *Star Trek* was a disaster and an embarrassment. Fortunately for his future recognizability, he thought better of this idea.

Still, one obstacle remained to be overcome. The makeup department had yet to come up with a painless means of applying the Spock ears. The ears were irritating and painful where the glue was applied; one of the reasons for Spock's general stiffness was the fact that any facial movement, however slight, served only to compound the intense physical discomfort generated by the aural appliances.

Matters were even more confounded by the odd fact that, due to contractual obligations, the actual ears had to be made by the props department, not the makeup department. Considerable variations in the shape of the ears (as well as in Spock's general appearance) can still be seen in the two pilot episodes. Leonard was frustrated by this situation, and expressed his dissatisfaction over it to his producer.

Roddenberry could tell that Nimoy's anguish was real—but what could he do? Finally, grasping at straws, he promised Nimoy that if, after thirteen episodes, he was still unhappy with the ears, Roddenberry would personally write an episode in which Spock had an ear-job to give him normal, human-looking ears. Nimoy pondered this, and then broke into laughter. The fate of the ears was sealed—and Spock still has them to this day.

"The Cage" introduces viewers to Roddenberry's nascent version of the *Enterprise* crew as it is headed toward a starbase after a disastrous first contact with an alien culture. Captain Pike and his crew are tired and in great need of some rest, but they are distracted by a distress signal from a nearby planet.

When they investigate, they find a colony of scientists who have survived a crash nearly twenty years earlier . . . and a beautiful young girl, Vina, who the survivors claim was born just as their ship crashed. When Vina lures Captain Pike away from the encampment, he is abducted by dome-skulled aliens and taken below the surface. The scientists and their camp, merely an illusion designed to lure humans, disappear.

Pike regains consciousness to find himself in an enclosed space; he has become part of an alien zoo, held prisoner by beings who can read his thoughts and project him into a bewildering variety of subjective but real-seeming scenarios. As he goes through these, he resists them at every turn, but begins to realize that the girl has a role in all this, too. Perhaps she is not an illusion, but another captive; she constantly tries to get him to accept his situation and make the best of the illusions his captors create.

Meanwhile, Number One and Spock haul out an impressive array of technology in their attempts to free their captain from his subterranean prison, but to no avail. Beneath the surface, the philosophical drama unfolds, with Pike finally being freed after resisting mind control. It is revealed that the woman, Vina, was the only survivor of the crash; not truly young, she was also severely disfigured by the crash. When Pike offers to take her off the planet to rejoin humanity, she elects to stay and live the rest of her life in the illusionary happiness the aliens have provided her. The aliens have been acting partly out of their own motivations but also out of a desire to help the lonely woman. Pike goes on to a starbase while she continues to embrace a reality that is false but which offers her the only comfort she will ever know.

NBC's reaction to this pilot was overwhelmingly enthusiastic. In its intelligence and its appearance, it surpassed anything done in the genre television before, and looked better than the vast majority of theatrical science fiction films as well. No one had a bad word to say about the finished product.

They rejected it anyway.

The problem, it seemed, was that it was *too* intelligent. NBC execs were afraid that the story would go over the heads of most of the audience. Something a bit more action-oriented would perhaps be better, they mused— and, in an unprecedented move, they gave Roddenberry a shot at a second pilot.

They also wanted to get rid of the guy with the pointed ears. There was always the possibility that religious groups might be offended by such a demonic-looking character.

Roddenberry set out to revamp the entire show, but he was determined to keep Spock. He discarded the character of Number One, who hadn't gone over too well, and promoted Spock to second-in-command, bringing him closer to the forefront.

This time, NBC wanted three complete scripts for consideration. All three had plenty of action: "Mudd's Women," by Stephen Kandel; "Omega Glory," by Roddenberry; and "Where No Man Has Gone Before," by Samuel A. Peeples. The network chose the Peeples script; the second *Star Trek* pilot was under way.

CHAPTER TWO:

A NEAR MISS AND A SOLID HIT

espite the network's misgivings, Roddenberry was determined to stick with Spock. He was also determined to maintain the *Enterprise*'s multiethnic crew despite the network's concerns that this might affect ratings in various areas of the country.

As for Spock, Roddenberry worked with the character a bit; the now-discarded Number One left a vacancy for the second-in-command, and Spock fit the bill perfectly. Spock also inherited Number One's cold, dispassionate logic. This all gelled to provide a fascinating amalgam of intelligence, restraint, and a certain attractive aura of mystery, all admirably brought to life by a highly capable actor, Leonard Nimoy.

Leonard Nimoy was born in Boston in 1931, the son of Jewish immigrants from the USSR. He showed an early interest in the theater, making his stage debut in a production of *Hansel and Gretel* at the age of eight.

After high school, he studied briefly at Boston College. With only six hundred dollars to his name, he took a three-day train trip to California in pursuit of an acting career. Studies at the Pasadena Playhouse did not lead to much movie work, however, and he was obliged to work at a variety of menial jobs: theater usher, ice cream counterman, pet shop clerk, vacuum cleaner salesman, and many others.

A fluke break landed him the lead in a Z-grade boxing picture, *Kid Monk Baroni,* but this and a few much smaller roles in such forgettable pictures as *Francis Goes to West Point,* where he was billed far below the picture's talking-donkey star, were all the film work he could obtain at the time.

After marriage and a stint in the army in Georgia, Nimoy returned to Los Angeles in the late fifties and began to get more roles in episodic television, frequently as a heavy. But he was far from being a household name.

In fact, although it was too early to realize it, it was his fortuitous encounter with Gene Roddenberry and *The Lieutenant* series that would save him from a career as one of those all-too-familiar faces whose name the audience can't quite place. *Star Trek* would soon preclude this possibility from ever coming true.

With Nimoy the sole holdover from "The Cage" pilot, Roddenberry was obliged to create an entirely new cast from scratch. Of course, the most important character on any ship is the captain. Inspired by C. S. Forester's heroic Horatio Hornblower character, Roddenberry created a new leader for the *Enterprise,* James Tiberius Kirk.

Kirk, a Midwesterner, is a driven officer with great faith in himself, who is not afraid to take a stand; apart from his senior officers, he confides in few, and bears the full responsibility for his command. Yet he is not without humor and he has a highly developed sense of adventure. For this all-important lead role, Roddenberry cast actor William Shatner.

William Shatner, thirty-eight at the time he started playing Captain Kirk, was born in Canada and was, like Leonard Nimoy, involved in the theater quite early. By the time he graduated McGill University in 1952, Shatner had already done extensive radio acting work.

He then joined the National Repertory Theater of Ottawa, where he earned the massive sum of thirty-one dollars (Canadian) a week. After years of hard work he received excellent reviews in a New York production of *Tamburlaine,* but he turned down a seven-year, five-hundred-dollar-a-week (American) contract with Twentieth Century-Fox in order to return to Canada and star in a television drama that he had written himself.

Soon afterward, he returned to New York and became extremely active in live television. He also played in the movie *The Brothers Karamazov,* which starred Yul Brynner. Work in westerns soon followed. He settled in Los Angeles, determined to make his fortunes in Hollywood.

Roles on *The Twilight Zone* and *Outer Limits* feature prominently in his resume from this period. He starred in the classic *Twilight Zone* episode "Nightmare at 20,000 Feet," and in the *Outer Limits* episode "Cold Hands, Warm Heart" he delivered, at one point, a passionate declaration about the importance of space exploration which sounds like a paraphrase of the opening narration of every *Star Trek* episode.

For the technical end of things, Roddenberry came up with the character of the chief engineer, Montgomery Scott. A regular shirtsleeves kind of guy, with an unbending devotion to his captain superseded only by his devotion to his ship, Scott would often be called upon to do the impossible, in as little time as he could manage. His ethnic background was suggested by the actor who played Scott. He was gifted in the area of dialects, and since there was a long tradition of Scotsmen in nautical and military engineering, his suggestion was approved.

Star Trek's other Canadian, James Doohan, was born in Vancouver, British Columbia, and flew an artillery observation plane in the Royal Canadian Air Force during the Second World War. Like many other actors of his generation, he did extensive radio work. He arrived in the United States in 1946 and remained until 1953, performing and teaching acting.

In 1961 he came back to the United States and worked on such television shows as *Bonanza, Gunsmoke, Bewitched,* and *The FBI.* Doohan had been offered the role of the chief engineer on *Voyage to the Bottom of the Sea* right after he auditioned for *Star Trek,* and only a call from the *Star Trek* offices at just the right time decided him on which series he would take. Of Scotty, Doohan once surmised that perhaps his accent was not natural, but was actually learned, possibly in a time when people would re-create archaic modes of speech in order to reduce the monotony of an ever-more-homogeneous language. An intriguing theory, indeed!

For the helmsman, who also doubles as weapons officer, Roddenberry created a character of Asian background, Sulu, who is primarily Japanese but also has Filipino blood. Sulu was portrayed by George Takei.

George Takei was born in Los Angeles but spent the World War Two period in Arkansas where, as a child, he lived with his family in a Japanese/American detention camp. He studied architecture at U.C. Berkeley and earned a bachelor's degree at UCLA in 1960.

In the few years between this and the debut of *Star Trek,* he managed to appear on a number of shows, including *Perry Mason* and *I Spy.* He also acted in *The Green Berets, The Brothers Karamazov,* and other movies.

He appeared in *The Twilight Zone* episode "The Encounter," an episode no longer included in the syndication package for reasons of anti-Japanese prejudice expressed in the script.

At a time when the networks were still dubious about the use of black characters in television (Bill Cosby's equal billing with Robert Culp on *I Spy* was definitely the exception, not the rule), Roddenberry pushed the envelope by creating the black communications officer Uhura.

Things were thrown more out of kilter when he made the character a woman as well. Even after the loss of the Number One character, he was determined to have a woman in a responsible position on the *Enterprise* bridge. In this, he was years ahead of our own military.

Uhura, whose name means "freedom," was from an African nation (according to the background material, anyway), and is proof of the changes Earth society has achieved in Roddenberry's hopeful vision of the future.

Actress, dancer, and singer Nichelle Nichols was cast as Uhura. Born in Chicago, she had worked extensively as a vocalist, and toured with Duke Ellington's and Lionel Hampton's bands. On stage, she appeared in such plays as *The Blacks, No Strings, Carmen Jones,* and James Baldwin's *Blues for Mister Charlie.*

With the new cast set and ready to go, "Where No Man Has Gone Before" started shooting on July 21, 1965, and was not completed until January 1966, costing $330,000 to produce. Needless to say, the network was eager to see what it had been waiting for.

Roddenberry and his team were on tenterhooks; would NBC reject this effort, too? In February, the word came through: *Star Trek* would debut in December, with the network committed to sixteen episodes. It was time to start producing the series. With a budget of roughly $180,000 an episode, it was going to be quite a ride.

Early on, the idea of incorporating the rejected "Cage" pilot into a two-part episode was put forward as a means of relieving the expected time-and-budget crunch. Set building, prop design, and, of course, scripts all occupied a great deal of this preparation period.

Roddenberry attended the World Science Fiction Convention in Cleveland on September 4, 1966, where he showed "Where No Man Has Gone Before" to a suitably impressed audience of five hundred die-hard science fiction fans.

"Where No Man Has Gone Before" was different from the form that *Star Trek* would soon assume. Uhura had not yet joined the roster, nor had Yeoman Janice Rand; the ship's doctor, Dr. Piper, was portrayed by Paul Fix; and Sulu was a physicist, not the helmsman. Several characters in key roles appeared only in the pilot.

What the Worldcon audience saw was the story of how the *Enterprise* tries to penetrate a mysterious purple energy barrier in space. Strange radiations affect the crew; Lieutenant Commander Gary Mitchell seems normal, but his eyes begin to glow silver. It soon becomes apparent that the radiation has boosted his latent extrasensory perceptions to a previously undreamed-of level. Mitchell's mental powers begin to accelerate, and Spock becomes convinced that Mitchell is a threat to the *Enterprise* and prompts Kirk to kill him.

But the Captain cannot bring himself to terminate an old college buddy from Starfleet Academy. Ultimately, Kirk and Mitchell battle to the death in a harsh landscape altered by Mitchell's godlike powers. At one point, Mitchell produces a tombstone bearing the name of James R. Kirk, proving that even a nearly omnipotent being can get someone's middle initial wrong. Finally, Kirk destroys Mitchell, but it is a hollow triumph, as he has killed the friend he once had.

The audience gave Roddenberry a standing ovation; he knew then that he was on the right track.

Finally, on September 8, 1966, *Star Trek* premiered on NBC. (Actually, the first broadcast was two days earlier, on Canadian television.) The episode aired was not the pilot (that was shown two weeks later) but the sixth episode filmed, "The Man Trap," perhaps best known for its piteous Salt Vampire nemesis.

This episode was most notable for introducing audiences to a character who was not actually in the pilot, but who would quickly become an indispensable part of the *Star Trek* myth: Dr. Leonard "Bones" McCoy.

This seemingly cynical but strongly compassionate humanitarian would provide a constant counterpoint to the cold logic of Spock, and their battle of wits would soon become legendary.

Fed up with protocol, distrustful of technology (especially transporters), and wary of dehumanizing influences, in a way McCoy represents the probable reaction of an intelligent twentieth-century man cast forward into the twenty-third century. He has his roots very much in our present. Veteran actor DeForest Kelley was called upon to bring this crucial character to life.

DeForest Kelley was born in Atlanta, but bucked his Baptist minister father's desire for him to become a doctor and opted for acting instead. Moving to Long Beach, California, he continued the radio work he had begun in Georgia, and also worked as an elevator operator.

In the navy during World War Two, he worked in training films, where he was spotted by a talent scout from Paramount. He worked as a contract player at Paramount Studios for two and a half years. About this time, a fortune-teller told him that he would not achieve success until after he passed the age of forty, which proved to be true!

Then, in 1948, he went to New York City and worked in television and on stage. Returning to Hollywood, he worked extensively in westerns, both on television shows such as *Gunsmoke, Rawhide,* and *Bonanza* and in movies such as *Gunfight at the O.K. Corral* and *Warlock.* For

Gene Roddenberry, Kelley starred in two pilots: 1960's *Free, Free, Free Montgomery*, in which he played a famous, controversial defense attorney named Jake Early, and the unsold *Police Story* (no relation to the later TV series).

With the key elements in place and the show finally in production and on the air, *Star Trek* was now more than a dream in Gene Roddenberry's mind. It was a reality. *Variety* insisted that the series wouldn't work; time has certainly proven the newspaper wrong.

CHAPTER THREE:

ONWARD TO THE STARS, WITH HOPE

(THE FIRST SEASON)

A week before *Star Trek* premiered, the *Buffalo Evening News* previewed new shows:

> A 400-man space ship, the U.S.S. *Enterprise*, cruises the TV universe this fall starting Thursday night in *Star Trek,* NBC's expensive full-hour science fiction adventure series about puny man exploring the wide blue yonder. Starring the talented Canadian actor William Shatner as spaceship commander Kirk, assisted by brainy, elf-eared Mr. Spock (Leonard Nimoy), *Star Trek* goes back and forth in time, jousting with alien spirits, bewildering viruses and ordinary human conflicts on a never-ending trip to other worlds.

In this article, both NBC and Shatner are already defending the show against criticism, days before it even premieres. NBC tries to cast *Star Trek* as action/adventure rather than science fiction. At a time when *Bonanza* was a hit and science fiction television was represented by *Lost in Space,* their concern was well-founded! Shatner insists, "We're not going to be like the children's show *Lost in Space,* where characters battle villains in eerie costumes. . . . We deal with human conflicts against a science fiction background." Some of these conflicts will include Kirk's Jekyll and Hyde battle with his own self, the attack of a bizarre virus that robs humans of will, and Mr. Spock's battle to be a true Vulcan and control his feelings.

Star Trek promises to deliver new and exotic technology, fun gadgets, and wild special effects:

> The Earth men have a few dandy tools and gadgets on display, all calculated to catch the fancy of young viewers. Captain Kirk and crew make excellent use of laser beam guns, jolting enemies with the sizzle of cutting light. They listen and understand various alien languages by way of walkie-talkie interpreters that translate foreign words in a split second.

From these clumsy attempts to describe *Star Trek*'s technology, it would have been hard to imagine that much of its terminology would actually one day be incorporated into common daily usage. The only clue is that according to Shatner, there is already a company working on a real-life walkie-talkie interpreter! "That's the point of our show—science fiction projections into the future based on what is possible today."

The *Buffalo Evening News* places *Star Trek* a step above *Lost in Space* and *Voyage to the Bottom of the Sea,* but calls it a *Twilight Zone* set in space. Of course, a show this new would be hard to categorize—Roddenberry even once tried to sell the idea as a space western!

The *News* comes out in praise of Shatner, both for his bold plugs for the new show and for his previous acting credits, including Shakespeare, Broadway, and the short-lived TV series *For the People*. Fortunately for the actor, the new show would enjoy a longer TV life than his first effort; in fact, it would make him world-famous.

"The Man Trap," written by *Twilight Zone* alumnus George Clayton Johnson, kicked off the *Star Trek* series with a story featuring Dr. McCoy's apparent reunion with his old flame Nancy, now married to archaeologist Robert Crater. Unfortunately, Nancy is actually dead and is being impersonated by a creature that lives off the body salt of other living creatures.

Things are further compounded by its ability to take on any form. McCoy is faced with the agonizing truth in a story that is quite poignant and moving. The good doctor's futuristic medical supplies came out of the prop search for this episode, as futuristic salt shakers were sought out but then discarded for fear that they wouldn't be recognized as such. The props department, always on a budget, converted the salt shakers into medical devices.

The next episode aired, "Charlie X," featured Robert Walker, Jr., as a space foundling whose hidden psychic powers are ill matched with his adolescent need for attention and approval, in a story about loneliness and alienation. In hindsight, the story has more than passing similarities to the central character in Robert Heinlein's 1961 novel *Stranger in a Strange Land*.

"Where No Man Has Gone Before" was the third episode broadcast.

Things really hit their stride with "The Naked Time," which gave the *Star Trek* cast a chance to show off their range when an alien microbe opens up the ship's crew to their innermost personal conflicts. Kirk's love of the *Enterprise* wars with his knowledge that the command keeps him from having a normal life. Spock's dual heritage leads to even more divided behavior, and he is seen to actually weep.

The ship, meanwhile, finds itself in danger of being destroyed, but is saved through the simple expedient of a little minor time travel, the first for the series. This episode also introduces Nurse Christine Chapel and her unrequited love for the unreachable Mr. Spock.

"The Enemy Within" gives Shatner a shot at strutting his stuff when a transporter malfunction divides him into two diametrically opposed selves. Believe it or not, this episode first explored on television the much-abused concept of the "evil twin," and this is perhaps the only time on TV that it was ever explored with any thought or imagination. Hack TV writers reduced the idea to a trivial cliché in the seventies and eighties on countless television shows.

"Mudd's Women," one of the three scripts proposed for the second pilot submission, introduces Roger C. Carmel as the rascally space swindler Harry Mudd. This also marks the first time the *Enterprise* is in dire need of fresh dilithium crystals. Furthermore, Mudd actually gives another character a pleasure drug—a fact overlooked by the network censor!

On October 15, 1966 (two days after "Mudd's Women"), *TV Guide* featured a profile of William Shatner. Entitled "No One Ever Upsets The STAR," it details Shatner's first taste of real fame.

William Shatner, *Star Trek*'s 35-year-old Montreal-born ex-Hollywood holdout, sits in his plush Desilu dressing room force-feeding himself on five pages of rush dialogue. He is interrupted first by a small man bearing a new-style jacket on a hanger, and then an intently solicitous press agent, and then an eager-to-please youth who asks in the manner of a bellhop addressing the man in the presidential suite, "Would you like something cold to drink?"

Shatner appears to love all this attention, and comments on his new attitude, "Before, I always thought that kind of, uh, toadying was beneath human dignity. But for the first time I'm able to see the reason for it. These little attentions do help. It makes life easier for me." Later he continues, "I've gotten great insight into the omnipotence of the series lead. Everybody does his best not to upset the star. It's an almost unique position few in the entertainment world achieve . . . it's like absolute power."

Shatner then joins Leonard Nimoy, already wearing his famous ears, guest star Robert Walker, Jr., and director Larry Dobkin for a rehearsal just outside his dressing room. Shatner insists on these off-the-set run-throughs, an innovation that earns him the applause of most of the directors. The actor evidently has firm ideas about the show itself, and when an associate producer arrives with late, late script changes, Shatner gets testy. (Later, he persuades Roddenberry to outlaw these last-minute changes.)

Not content just to be the star, Shatner from the beginning would approach Roddenberry with his comments about the script. Later, he presented Gene with a script he himself had written. Roddenberry was impressed—"I caught myself wishing I could write that well. . . ."—but not inspired to buy the script. Working with such an assertive actor at first seemed ominous, "but it wasn't so bad. I have never had more intelligent suggestions, and we used all of them," Roddenberry said.

Shatner took to stardom like a natural from the very first, and in the years since that first season, he has even realized his early dream of writing and directing.

"What Are Little Girls Made Of?" again features two Kirks (Shatner must have loved this!) when he is duplicated, in android form, by Nurse Chapel's fiancé, Dr. Roger Korby. She's been searching for him, but he seems to have gone just a little bit 'round the bend, and is intent on taking over the *Enterprise* and populating the universe with his androids, one of whom, Ruk, is portrayed by Ted Cassidy (Lurch on *The Addams Family*). This episode has a strange, eerie quality about it, and writer Robert Bloch, who wrote the novel on which the film *Psycho* was based, peppers it with arcane references to aspects of H. P. Lovecraft's mythos. Kirk's brother George is mentioned in this episode.

"Miri" brings Kirk and crew to a planet remarkably like Earth, where ancient children live long lives until their long-delayed puberty causes them to sicken and die. Kirk is beaten up by children in this episode; McCoy finds a cure for the aging disease before almost succumbing to it himself.

"Dagger of the Mind" involves Kirk's discovery of the abuses of power at a supposedly humane penal colony. This introduces the Vulcan mind meld, which conveniently serves as a means to avoid a lengthy expository conversation with a mentally deranged character.

"The Corbomite Maneuver" was actually the third episode filmed, as well as being the first one to include McCoy as a character. Here Kirk encounters a massive, threatening spaceship that is not what it seems to be.

The next two broadcasts consisted of a two-parter, "The Menagerie," which incorporated much of the footage from the first pilot, "The Cage." Here Spock goes to great lengths to take Captain Pike, crippled in an accident, back to Talos IV so that he can live out his life in a happy illusion created by the Talosians. Through flashbacks, Spock explains his actions to Kirk and the others.

By this point in the series, one thing was crystal clear:

Mr. Spock, originally a supporting character, was becoming as popular as the lead, Captain Kirk. At times, Shatner even felt obliged to remind some series scriptwriters that *he* was the captain; he later acknowledged that there was sometimes friction between him and Leonard, but made certain to indicate that this was a thing of the past: "We went through that fire together and today we are fast friends. Leonard is an honest man and a fine craftsman." Still, at the time Shatner was so concerned over the situation that he counted his lines in each new script to be certain that he had more than Nimoy. If he didn't, either more were added for him at his insistence, or some of Nimoy's lines were cut.

Norman Spinrad once related the story of his visit to the set of the episode he had scripted, "The Doomsday Machine." He witnessed the director trying to come up with an alternative way for Nimoy to react to Shatner in a scene because for Nimoy to utter a line would have given him one line too many, as far as Shatner was concerned.

But by the end of 1966, *Star Trek* was already in trouble. NBC was dissatisfied with the Nielsen ratings, and was, as usual, uncertain of how to categorize the series. The show had already generated a highly positive response in the science fiction subculture, of course, and so Roddenberry turned to Harlan Ellison for help. Perhaps if the network knew just how large an audience science fiction fandom represented, it might very well see the show in a new light.

And so, Ellison sent out five thousand letters urging science fiction fans to press NBC with a letter-writing campaign. Dated December 1, 1966, Ellison's missive bore the letterhead of "The Committee," an impressive listing of names: Paul Anderson, Robert Bloch, Lester Del Rey, Ellison, Philip Jose Farmer, Frank Herbert, Richard Matheson, Theodore Sturgeon, and A. E. Van Vogt. Thus Ellison, who would later be less than keen on his involvement with *Star Trek* ("The City on the Edge of Forever" had yet to be filmed), was in fact responsible for the very first letter campaign organized to benefit the series.

This, of course, was in the days when the Nielsen ratings presupposed a bland, all-encompassing uniformity belonging to the "average" TV viewer. With this sort of a priori approach, it is hardly surprising that the appeal of *Star Trek* did not dovetail with the Nielsen company's concepts, and hence eluded its comprehension. But in those pre-demographics days, before the variety of the American mind-set was taken into consideration, the Nielsen ratings were the voice of God as far as the networks were concerned. Those were the numbers that determined a show's advertising value and marketability, as well as its popularity, despite whatever evidence reality had to offer to the contrary.

And evidence there was. The stars of *Star Trek* had become wildly popular with the public . . . almost, if not quite, overnight. The ratings problem seems almost ironic when held up against this fact.

In 1966, Leonard Nimoy and William Shatner were invited to appear in Hollywood's annual Christmas parade. This newfound fame was no guarantee of respect, however, for while the parade announcer got Shatner's name correct, he introduced the other *Star Trek* star as "Leonard Nimsy." Despite this gaffe, Nimoy was, for the first time in his life, frequently recognized on the street, and constantly besieged for autographs.

He took it all in good humor, although he soon became weary of smart-aleck fans asking him where he'd left his ears. Fan mail began to pour in, too, a great deal of it from younger viewers.

All of this was uncharted territory for Nimoy. At first, he was determined to answer all his fan mail by himself. Thirty or so letters a week was no big deal, after all.

Unfortunately for this plan, the numbers began to increase every week, until thousands of messages were pouring in. He had to hire an assistant, Teresa Victor, to help him cope with his popularity. The other *Star Trek* stars made similar arrangements.

With the success of the show, the principal actors were better off financially than they had been in their entire careers. Nimoy used this money to upgrade his personal transportation, and replaced his battered old car with a new Buick luxury auto. Shatner went for something sportier, while DeForest Kelley bought a Thunderbird—which he managed to ram into Nimoy's Buick one day at the end of shooting. Things proceeded amicably, but passersby were probably a bit nonplussed to see a normal-looking man exchanging insurance information with Leonard, who was still rigged up in full Spock regalia.

There was also a downside to Nimoy's newfound celebrity. Early in *Star Trek*'s run, NBC arranged for him to be the grand marshal of Medford, Oregon's annual Pear Blossom Festival; this was to be his first real promotional trip, and he was quite unprepared for the chaos that would surround it. The parade went without a hitch—but it had also been announced that Nimoy would sign autographs in a small park at the end of the parade route. A crowd, with a large number of young people, actually followed Leonard's itinerary. By the time he reached the park, it was swarming with immense numbers of people. The lone park employee was swamped by this madness; traffic was completely fouled up. In the end, Medford police had to make their way in and "rescue" Nimoy from the friendly mob.

Eventually, it reached the point where people actually turned down the chance for a Spock/Nimoy appearance. Macy's, the famous New York department store, declined to have Nimoy appear to promote one of his record albums. The stone honestly admitted that it could not handle the sort of crowds which would undoubtedly attend such an event.

Nimoy himself turned down many requests for public appearances because they asked for him to wear the ears in public; he estimated losing about fifty thousand dollars in passing up these offers.

His popularity continued to manifest itself in a bewildering variety of ways. Spock was the only *Star Trek* character to merit solo reproduction as a model kit. While Kirk and Sulu did join Spock as small figures in AMT's *Enterprise* Bridge model, a six-inch-tall Spock was featured in a larger diorama kit that featured him facing off against a three-headed alien serpent. (In 1975, Spock and other *Star Trek* characters would have the dubious honor of being reproduced as ice pop molds!)

His face also appeared on a variety of series-related toy packages over the years, including original show style phaser rifles and the ever-popular *Star Trek* disc gun. "I Grok Spock" buttons, alluding to Robert Heinlein's classic 1961 science fiction novel *Stranger in a Strange Land,* began to crop up as well.

By this point, the NBC executives who had wanted to give Spock the axe were now acting as if they'd been for the character all along. Leonard's place in the public consciousness was rock-solid, and the first season wasn't even over yet!

"The Conscience of the King" involves Kirk in efforts to determine whether a well-known Shakespearian actor is actually the man responsible for a massacre some years earlier; Kirk is one of the few survivors. An intriguing study of guilt and self-punishment, with an intriguing plot twist or two, it is ably supported by actor Arnold Moss in a very demanding role.

"Balance of Terror" introduces the Romulans, who have returned after a century to harass the Federation with the assistance of their new cloaking devices. This story, essentially a submarine movie set in space, featured Mark Lenard as the Romulan commander. Lenard would, of course, play Spock's father Sarek in a future episode.

"Shore Leave," written by Theodore Sturgeon, prefigures the movie *Westworld* by some years, as the crew beams down for R&R on a planet that seems to be deadly but is actually an artifact programmed to custom-tailor amusements for each individual. This marks the first time a leading *Star Trek* character dies, only to return intact. (This time around it's McCoy.)

"The Galileo Seven" brings Spock to the forefront as he commands a shuttlecraft which crashes, leaving him, Scotty, and Dr. McCoy stranded on a hostile planet. Is his logic sufficient to save the castaways, or must he learn to look at things from an irrational perspective?

"The Squire of Gothos" is Trelane, who traps the *Enterprise* and her crew to be his playthings; he is a powerful, godlike being, but also a child, ultimately answerable to his parents . . . though not before shaking up the resolute Captain Kirk a bit.

"Arena" adapts the classic science fiction story by Fredric L. Brown and casts Kirk in the lead, as the captain and the lizardlike Gorn are chosen as champions of their respective races by the meddlesome superior Metrons.

"Tomorrow Is Yesterday" is the first solid time-travel story for *Star Trek,* in which the *Enterprise* is hurled back to the twentieth century by the gravitational field of a black hole. Matters are complicated when an air force jet spots the *Enterprise* and Kirk must decide what to do with pilot John Christopher.

In "Court Martial," Captain Kirk is tried for criminal negligence which resulted in the death of an officer; the redoubtable Mr. Spock applies his logic to the case and ultimately proves that the officer is really alive, having staged his own death in order to satisfy a personal grudge against Kirk.

Sulu gets to go nuts on-screen in "The Return of the Archons," in which the *Enterprise* investigates the planet Beta III, which is ruled by a mysterious computer. (The last Federation ship to visit, a century earlier, was called the *Archon*; hence the returning Archons of the title are Kirk and his crew.) The outsiders are threatened with absorption, but Kirk ultimately talks the ancient computer into destroying itself. Spock actually hits someone in this episode.

"Space Seed" introduces Ricardo Montalban as Khan, a late-twentieth-century fanatic who, with his followers, has been adrift in a "sleeper ship" for hundreds of years. The *Enterprise* revives the sleepers only to be taken over by Khan, who uses the infatuation of Marla McGivers, a young woman officer, to gain control by cutting off the air to the bridge. At the end he is defeated (Kirk retaliates with knockout gas in the ventilation system) and chooses exile on an unexplored planet for himself and his people. McGivers chooses to join him.

"A Taste of Armageddon" draws Kirk into a peculiar war between the planets Eminiar Seven and Vendikar: battles are no longer fought, but computers do the fighting and determine the casualties. Victims in the affected areas then willingly report for euthanasia.

Kirk is appalled by this, of course—and all the more so when the *Enterprise* is decreed a casualty of war. Kirk and crew destroy the computers and leave the two worlds faced with the options of real war on the one hand and peaceful negotiations on the other.

"This Side of Paradise" takes the *Enterprise* to a colony that should have died of radiation poisoning years earlier, but survived because of spores on the planet Omicron Ceti III that also provide a constant sense of euphoria. The crew all fall prey to this, rendering them unfit for (and uninterested in) their duties. Foremost among these is Spock, who once again has his emotions liberated, as in "The Naked Time." He falls in love with a young botanist whom he had known before. Kirk must discover a way to get his crew back; Spock's happy romance is unfortunately short-lived. (He is also referred to as a Vulcanian on the show for the first and last time, since the terminology still hadn't been standardized!)

About this time, in its issue of March 4, 1967, *TV Guide* featured a profile of Leonard Nimoy.

> It could only happen in America: where else could a son of Russian immigrants become a television star with pointed ears?

The article then describes the picture of the "Spock Cut" in Max Nimoy's Boston barber shop, where he would proudly point out his son to all customers; Nimoy's mother, Dora, was sometimes interrupted at her job in a department store by people wanting to look at Spock's mother.

According to *TV Guide,* much of Leonard Nimoy's fan mail was from younger viewers, who thought Spock was "cool." Roddenberry had a more philosophical idea: "We're all imprisoned within ourselves. We're all aliens on this strange planet, so people find identification with Spock." Since it was the 1960s, it's no surprise that so many young people felt they had more in common with a Vulcan than with their own parents!

Some fans had other ideas, and to many Spock became a sex symbol. A drama school colleague, actress Evelyn Ward, believed Nimoy's own "great animal magnetism" was the reason for Spock's popularity. Hidden for years under the heavy makeup of his Native American and Mexican roles, Nimoy's charm was lying in wait for Gene Roddenberry's genius—and a pair of pointed ears—to bring it out.

Hero for youth or sex symbol, Leonard Nimoy

attempted to give Spock more depth and character. Spock was more than ears and eyebrows, largely because of Nimoy's attitude: "I don't want to play a creature or a computer. Spock gives me a chance to say something about the human race." From the start, Nimoy hoped that the Spock role would bring him bigger projects: "I have all sorts of things I want to do. Perhaps this show will give me the wherewithal to do some of them. " But for now, he said, "I'm having a ball. It's the first steady job I've had in seventeen years."

Offscreen, Nimoy looked pretty much like an ordinary guy, if you overlook the "Spock Cut." Quiet and serious, he even insisted that people call him Leonard, not "Lenny." Though nicknames are almost required on a set, Nimoy managed to preserve a truly Vulcan dignity, regardless of whether he was being Spock or just plain Leonard Nimoy.

"The Devil in the Dark" is the Horta, a silicon-based creature that has been killing miners in the underground colony of Janus VI. The *Enterprise* is called in on the crisis, but Spock discovers, by means of the Vulcan mind meld, that it is actually a mother protecting its young, in this case spherical eggs which had previously seemed only peculiar geological phenomena. The real conflict of this story is the need to overcome the fear and hostility of the human miners when they are faced with something new and incomprehensible.

The Horta costume, designed and worn by Janos Prohaska, was originally used in the last *Outer Limits* episode, "The Probe," but was customized and refurbished for its appearance on *Star Trek*.

"Errand of Mercy" sends Kirk to the peaceful, pastoral world of Organia, which is in danger of Klingon attack; Klingon/Federation relations have become increasingly strained, and war seems imminent. When Commander Kor and his Klingon force invade and take over, they

arrest Spock and Kirk, but the Organians themselves seem
unperturbed by the occupation. Still, the Organians rescue
Kirk and Spock, and avert war by the use of their previously unsuspected mental powers, which render all
weapons ineffective. They are in fact completely evolved
beings whose human forms were a disguise, and they
promise to keep a watchful eye on the enemy factions. In
spite of the major plot element represented by the
Organians and their ability to force an end to war, they
were never used again in any subsequent *Star Trek*
episode.

"The Alternative Factor" involves the battle between
Lazarus and his antimatter double Lazarus; the fate of the
universe hangs in the balance, and once again hinges on
the need for dilithium crystals.

"The City on the Edge of Forever" is generally
regarded as one of the best *Star Trek* episodes; it is also
perhaps the episode with the most interesting background
history. Harlan Ellison's original script was rewritten by
Gene Roddenberry, perhaps unnecessarily, and has
become a long-standing source of annoyance for the
writer. Roddenberry's reasons for the rewrite have
become somewhat clouded with the passage of time; he
has claimed that Ellison's script included huge crowd
scenes and other factors which would have drastically
exceeded the show's budget (not exactly true), and even
that the script had Scotty dealing drugs!

Ellison's original draft did hinge on a low-ranking
crew member dealing in illegal drugs, but it was not
Scotty by any means; perhaps Roddenberry was simply
aghast that someone might dare to show a seamy under-
side to his perfect human civilization of the future. The
script as written by Ellison was published in the now-
out-of-print *Six Science Fiction Plays,* edited by Roger
Ellwood, and is due to be published again soon . . . with an
extensive introduction by Ellison detailing the controversy

in all its gory details. But, despite Ellison's disavowals of the filmed product, his original story still shines through Roddenberry's rewrite, and the story retains its fascination.

In the story as filmed, Dr. McCoy accidentally injects himself with a powerful experimental drug and becomes completely unhinged. (Apparently Roddenberry would rather impugn the good doctor's basic competency than allow the blame to fall on a dishonest drug-smuggling crewman.) Meanwhile, Kirk and Spock are investigating a mysterious time portal, the Guardian of Forever, on the planet below.

McCoy beams down and leaps through the portal, disappearing into the past; the *Enterprise* suddenly ceases to exist, leaving Kirk and Spock stranded in a distant corner of the universe. They must go to the past and undo whatever it is McCoy has done to disrupt history. In 1930s New York, Kirk falls in love with Edith Keeler (Joan Collins), not realizing that she is the key to their predicament.

Spock manages to create a time-scanning device with his tricorder and the primitive technology of the period, and ultimately discovers that Keeler will, if she lives, lead a pacifist movement that will keep the USA out of World War Two. The Nazis will win the war and make history on Earth a veritable hell; thus, Keeler's humanitarian impulses contain the seeds of humanity's destruction.

Kirk must then force himself to keep the still delirious McCoy from saving Edith from her death under the wheels of a car. History is restored to its proper form— but not without some wrenching decisions for Kirk.

This was to be DeForest Kelley's favorite episode of the series. According to him, Edith was to have been the key character, but the story was rewritten to give McCoy a greater role.

"Operation: Annihilate!" features William Shatner in a

second role: that of the dead body of Kirk's older brother
George, complete with a mustache and gray hair. This
personal tragedy is discovered on the planet Deneva,
where alien parasites are attacking humans and driving
them to excruciatingly painful deaths. This episode's
effectiveness is somewhat enhanced by the fact that the
creatures look like enormous airborne fried eggs. Held to
a wall with electromagnets, these creatures fell to the
ground quite convincingly when hit by phaser fire.

This episode brought the first season to its end.
Leonard Nimoy would be nominated for Best Supporting
Actor in a Dramatic Series for this year's work.

Between seasons, in its issue of July 15, 1967, Nichelle
Nichols was profiled in *TV Guide.*

Although her presence on the show at all was considered daring, the actress felt strongly that her character was
too limited. She told *TV Guide,* "The producers admit
being very foolish and very lax in the way they've used
me—or not used me." Gene Coon, a producer, defended
Uhura's small role: "I thought it would be very ungallant
to imperil a beautiful girl with twenty-toed snaggle-
toothed monsters from outer space."

Nichols, however, did not feel imperiled by additional
dialogue, and by the end of the first season had increased
her dialogue quotient. No longer confined to "All hailing
frequencies open, sir," Nichols also began ad-libbing,
including the famous line, "Mr. Spock, if I have to say
'Hailing frequencies open' one more time, I'll blow my
top! Why don't you tell me I'm a lovely young woman?"

TV Guide saw this development as more important
than it turned out to be, alas, as borne out by a careful
examination of the seventy-nine known episodes of *Star
Trek.* But Roddenberry commented to *TV Guide* at the
time, "We're thinking about taking her down on the planets next season. Maybe we'll have wardrobe make her an
appropriate costume for planet wear." In fact, female

characters in addition to Uhura eventually beamed down to planets, still wearing the daring miniskirt uniform and getting involved in dangerous, often romantic, situations.

At the end of the first season, however, Nichols was so dismayed by her character's limitations that she considered quitting the show. But when she met civil rights leader Martin Luther King, Jr., he told her to stay with it; just appearing on the show as a bridge officer in a position of responsibility, he told her, she was providing a positive message that would be beneficial both to blacks and to the perception of blacks by others. (And somewhere in Brooklyn, the girl who would someday take the stage name of Whoopi Goldberg *was* inspired by Lieutenant Uhura.)

Of the famous tension between Spock and McCoy, DeForest Kelley tried to use elements of comedy and drama in the relationship, as related in a 1974 interview with Joseph Gulick:

> "I never wanted it thought for a minute that McCoy truly disliked [Spock]. McCoy had great respect for Spock, and I thought and felt that the best way was to somehow lighten it with an expression or a line. I did that purposefully. I didn't want to lose fans by being too hard with Spock under certain circumstances. McCoy liked him. It became a kind of battle of wits."

The on-screen battle of wits came about through hard work offscreen. Kelley and Nimoy discussed their scenes at great length, working on how they should be acted. According to Kelley, all the actors' deep caring for the show made for a unique taping situation. Unlike other shows, where actors would read a book or the trade papers between scenes, the crew of the *Enterprise* worked with the producer, breaking down future scenes and working on their parts—more like old-fashioned live New York television than Hollywood shows. Kelley explained, "This had a great bearing on the show. No one was out just running around or loafing or sleeping in a dressing room. They were preparing for the next scene."

Like the crew of the *Enterprise*, *Star Trek*'s cast often worked seven days, with grueling schedules often keeping them on the set until 8:30 or 9 P.M. That first season, Nimoy and Kelley reported for makeup around 6 A.M. Between their getting home at 10 P.M., then reporting back to the set at 6 A.M., a real starship crew may have had more time for R&R.

But by the second season the schedule had improved, and Kelley admits, "The first year was pure hell, but I think we did our best work in the first year when I look back."

CHAPTER FOUR:

STEADY AS SHE GOES

(THE SECOND SEASON)

uring the spring and summer of 1967, while the first season of *Star Trek* was in reruns, word began to spread that the next season would feature a visit to Spock's home planet, Vulcan. Needless to say, speculation was rife. That year in New York, World Science Fiction Convention attendees were the first to see the promised episode, "Amok Time," as well as the first season's blooper reel.

"Amok Time," written by veteran science fiction writer Theodore Sturgeon (who also wrote the first season's "Shore Leave"), proved to be well worth the wait. Keying in on the interest in Spock's emotional chinks, the story opened with the Vulcan officer acting decidedly strange and sulky.

McCoy determines that Spock will die if something is not done about the physical changes he's undergoing, and Spock admits, not to the doctor but to Kirk, that he is undergoing *Pon farr,* the Vulcan mating cycle, which will, indeed, be fatal if he doesn't get to Vulcan and undergo the proper rituals posthaste. Kirk bucks orders and reroutes the *Enterprise* to Vulcan.

The rituals involved are remnants of Vulcan's barbaric past (one wonders if they're really prudes except on these occasions). T'Pau, a dignified Vulcan leader, appears, as does the first use of the Vulcan ritual greeting "Live long and prosper." (Leonard Nimoy provided the accompanying hand gesture, which he "borrowed' from an important Jewish religious ritual; congregations were supposed to look away when the rabbi made this gesture, but Nimoy, as a young boy, couldn't help but peek!) Spock's would-be bride (by long-standing prearrangement, of course) T'Pring adds danger to the proceedings when she demands that Spock must engage in combat for her hand, and chooses Kirk as her champion. The fight must be to the death. Fortunately, McCoy manages to set up Kirk's "death" in order to end the fight. Spock snaps out of *Pon farr* thanks to this ruse, and is greatly relieved to find Kirk still alive; T'Pau gets Kirk out of any potential hot water by asking the Federation to divert the *Enterprise* to Vulcan.

Vulcan was presented here in sparse but effective visual terms; T'Pau, as portrayed by Peter Lorre's one-time wife Celia Lovsky, carries the entire implied culture in her bearing. Sturgeon provided many small but telling touches regarding ethics and customs of the planet Vulcan; photography and music added immensely to this episode. The Worldcon audience was suitably impressed.

The cast of *Star Trek* was altered to include a new character in the second season. The network was pressing for a character to rope in the "youth" market, something along the lines of Davy Jones of *The Monkees.* A press release (later revealed to have exaggerated the truth by fabricating the incident) claimed that the show was criticized by the Russian Communist newspaper *Pravda* for, among other things, its lack of a Russian character in the *Enterprise*'s otherwise multinational crew. And so to kill two birds with one stone, Roddenberry reportedly created the character of Ensign Pavel Chekov, a young officer with a heavy accent, to satisfy Soviet angst. Signing on as Chekov was actor Walter Koenig.

The second season of *Star Trek* began on September 15, 1967. The episode shown was "Amok Time," which also marked the first time DeForest Kelley received billing in the opening credits of the show.

"Who Mourns for Adonais?" brings the *Enterprise* into conflict with no less a personage than the Greek god Apollo, actually the last of a band of immortals who once visited Earth and lived on Mount Olympus. Scotty has a romantic interest here, but she falls for the god instead. Fortunately, Kirk manages to obtain her aid in destroying the temple that provides the god with his omnipotent powers, and Apollo destroys his own physical form and lets the *Enterprise* go. (In James Blish's adaptation of this episode, a final epilogue note from the original script is retained: the young woman is found to have become pregnant by the god Apollo.)

"The Changeling" is Nomad, an ancient Earth probe which has merged with an alien device and is convinced that its mission is to destroy imperfect life-forms. Unfortunately, humans fit its criteria perfectly. Fortunately, it thinks Kirk is the scientist Roykirk, the scientist who created it. Thus, out of deference to Kirk, it repairs Scotty after killing him. It is still a threat, but Kirk manages to trick it into destroying itself. (In retrospect, this seems to have been one of his specialties.)

"Mirror, Mirror" casts Kirk, McCoy, Scotty, and Uhura into an alternative universe where the Federation has developed along bloodthirsty, Klingonesque lines.

Meanwhile, their counterparts from the alternate universe arrive on the regular *Enterprise*, where Spock has the sense to toss them all in the brig. In the alternate universe, Kirk and crew meet, among others, a brutal and scarred Sulu, an ambitious Chekov, a "Captain's Woman," and a bearded Spock. Kirk uses logic to win Spock's assistance in his efforts to return home.

"The Apple" is the gift Kirk brings to the peaceful inhabitants of a dangerous world where their existence is protected by an ancient computer which also has retarded their social development. Kirk decides to violate Starfleet General Order Number One, known as the Prime Directive, which forbids Starfleet interference in a planet's domestic affairs. Kirk blows up the computer, saving the *Enterprise* but destroying the society of the planet, Gamma Trianguli VI.

"The Doomsday Machine" was shot from a script by Norman Spinrad and featured William Windom as Commodore Matthew Decker, the sole survivor of the crew of the U.S.S. *Constellation* (an AMT model kit, apparently "damaged" with a Zippo lighter). His crew was on a planet destroyed by the device of the title, which seems to be a planet-zapping weapon apparently built by a long-dead civilization. Decker, a latter-day Captain Ahab in space, is obsessed with destroying it, and hijacks the *Enterprise* to this end.

When Kirk regains control, Decker steals a shuttlecraft and dies trying to destroy the weapon. Kirk himself then flies the *Constellation* into the device's maw and sets it to self-destruct, transporting out in barely the nick of time and finishing off the device for good.

"Catspaw" was aired, appropriately enough, just before Halloween 1967 (on October 27, to be exact). Written by Robert Bloch, it involves the efforts of two shape-changing aliens to frighten the *Enterprise* crew with all the accoutrements of human superstition: magic, skeletons, witches, and the like. At one point, Kirk, Spock, and McCoy are chained in a dungeon; Kirk turns to address the doctor as "Bones," only to find a skeleton dangling in his friend's place. This macabre humor is further developed by Spock's inability (fortunate in these circumstances) to perceive any of the illusions thrown his way as frightening in any way, shape, or form. A final touch of pathos is introduced at the end when the aliens assume their true shapes and are found to be feeble, helpless creatures.

"I, Mudd" brings back Roger C. Carmel as Harry Mudd, currently serving as emperor of a planet of advanced androids. Of course, the androids realize what a buffoon he is, but they are using him to further their own plans of universal domination, which they intend to begin by stealing the *Enterprise*. Kirk and crew, including Spock, bewilder the androids by acting in absurd ways, and Mudd, who has created for himself a beautiful android harem, is punished by being afflicted with innumerable android replicas of the nagging, shrewish wife he'd abandoned long before.

"Metamorphosis" introduces Zefram Cochrane, the inventor of the warp drive, who was believed to have died a century before at the age of eighty-seven. It seems that he met a nebulous space creature who has kept him alive ever since; it has diverted the Galileo shuttlecraft to his location in order to provide him with human companionship. Cochrane begins to fall in love with the terminally ill Nancy Hedford, a Federation functionary who was being taken to the *Enterprise*. Kirk uses a translator to communicate with the alien companion and discovers that it is in love with Cochrane. Cochrane is initially repulsed by this, but accepts it when the immortal being merges with the dying woman, who stays with the scientist as the *Enterprise* resumes its course.

"Journey to Babel" finally introduces Spock's parents,

the Vulcan Sarek (Mark Lenard) and his human wife
Amanda (Jane Wyatt). The occasion is a diplomatic mission. A ship is following the *Enterprise*; the Tellarite
ambassador is murdered and Sarek is the prime suspect.
Sarek needs a blood transfusion for a heart operation, but
Spock must act as captain after an Andorian stabs Kirk.
Kirk fakes his recovery so Spock can give blood. A battle
with the ship results in its destruction. Kirk's attacker kills
himself after revealing that he killed the Tellarite ambassador, and Spock and his father achieve a rapprochement
after nearly twenty years of estrangement.

In December 1967, another letter campaign came to
the rescue of the again-beleaguered series. This one,
orchestrated by fan Bjo Trimble and her husband, John,
was even more successful than the first. Inspired by
NBC's decision to cancel the show, it generated an
unprecedented number of letters, and would prove instru-
mental in clearing the way for the show's third season.

New Year's Day, 1968, saw the *Star Trek* season's
continuation with a perhaps unintentional Christmas
touch: an episode wherein a child is born in a cave.

"Friday's Child" opens with a briefing on how to get
along in Capellan society. Kirk and crew are headed for
Capella IV to head off a potential alliance between that
world and the Klingons, but the good captain doesn't
seem to have learned much about the required protocol.
The planet's leader is deposed and his wife seems fated to
die, but Kirk interferes and the Klingons turn the Capellans
against him and his team. McCoy helps the woman deliver
her baby, who is ultimately named the new ruler when the
Klingons kill the latest ruler; the child is named "Leonard
James" after McCoy and Kirk—but Spock, not much for
children, it seems, gets short shrift.

"The Deadly Years" sees Kirk and his main officers
afflicted with a deadly disease that causes accelerated
aging. Spock ages the slowest, thanks to the longevity

of Vulcans, but McCoy's efforts to find a cure are hampered by his own senescence. A commodore on board convenes a hearing and removes the now nearly senile Kirk from command. He then takes the *Enterprise* right into the Neutral Zone, where a serious run-in with Romulans is averted through means of the old reliable Corbomite maneuver, executed by a Kirk restored to normalcy by McCoy's timely discovery of a remedy for the aging disease.

This rated as another of DeForest Kelley's favorite episodes. Again speaking to Joe Gulick in 1974, he observed: "I enjoyed doing ["The Deadly Years"] because it gave me an opportunity to do something that I would never be called upon to do." As his character aged, Kelley had him become more and more the old-fashioned country doctor McCoy really envisioned himself as. "Yes, I began to fall back. I had that in mind from the beginning, that the older he became, the more he would fall back into what he really had a feeling in his heart for. Fortunately, it worked very well. There was a great disturbance at the studio at the time, because they felt I should have been nominated for that show but I was not. They were very upset about it." Nimoy, however, would again receive an Emmy nomination for the second season.

In "Obsession," the *Enterprise* is attacked by a gaseous being that lives off human blood. Fortunately, the first crewman it attacks is Spock, and it flees, presumably with an unpleasant, copperlike taste in its "mouth." Kirk recognizes the creature as the one that destroyed half the crew of the U.S.S. *Farragut* over ten years before, when Kirk was a lieutenant on that vessel. The commander of the *Farragut*, Captain Garrovick, died in that encounter, but his son is now an ensign on the *Enterprise*. Kirk and Garrovick proceed to exorcise their pasts by tracking and destroying the monster.

"Wolf in the Fold" is Robert Bloch's third *Star Trek*

episode, adapted from Bloch's story "Yours Truly, Jack the Ripper," which was also adapted, more directly, in a 1961 episode of *Thriller* simply titled "The Ripper." The basic idea is that the Ripper is actually a long-lived being, but this at first is not revealed, as it is Scotty, recovering from a head injury, who is suspected of the horrible murders of several young women. Ultimately, the creature is exposed in its latest human form, and expelled into the depths of space. The phrase "He's dead, Jim" is used here an unsurpassed number of times.

"The Trouble with Tribbles" is a comic episode, in which a furry pet given to Lieutenant Uhura reproduces asexually at an alarming rate, threatening key *Enterprise* systems and delaying her famine relief mission to an endangered outpost. When tribbles start dying suddenly, the crew discovers that the emergency grain the creatures had been eating had been poisoned by Klingon spies. The outpost is saved from eating poisoned grain, and Scotty cleverly disposes of the nuisance creatures to the nearby Klingon ship, commenting that "They'll be no tribble at all."

"The Gamesters of Triskelion" are bored aliens who abduct Kirk, Chekov, and Uhura to take part in gladiatorial games for their own amusement. When the *Enterprise*, under Spock's command, reaches Triskelion, the ship is captured. Kirk makes a bet with the aliens and is set to fight Shahna, a beautiful woman. He wins the wager when it turns out that he has managed to teach her about human ideals (as well as about kissing), and the ship and crew, as well as the people of the planet, are freed. In an intriguing career move, Angelique Pettyjohn, who portrayed Shahna, later went on to star in various "adult" movies.

"A Piece of the Action" is another humorous episode in which Kirk discovers a civilization that has modeled itself on the society described in a book left by a

Federation mission one hundred years before: *Chicago Mobs of the Twenties*. Kirk is confounded by this situation until he decides to play along, and soon he and Spock are wearing pinstripes and fedoras and spouting variants of archaic Earth slang. Thus, Kirk finally succeeds in uniting the Iotians into a single government.

"The Immunity Syndrome" brings the *Enterprise* up against a giant space amoeba that must be destroyed; Spock and McCoy both vie for the chance to observe the creature firsthand in a shuttlecraft, but Spock earns this quite possibly fatal honor. Spock discovers that the creature is about to divide, and destroys it before its threat can be doubled. With his life support waning, he barely makes it back to the ship in time.

"A Private Little War" takes place on the planet Neural, where Klingons are providing arms to escalate a tribal conflict in preparation for their own invasion. Kirk must find someone he knew on his last visit to this world, the leader Tyree, but is attacked by a vicious Mugato, a horned yeti-like being, and becomes ill from its poison. Tyree's wife cures him but steals his phaser, only to be killed by the tribe backed by the Klingons. Tyree, reluctant to fight, is now determined to do so, and Kirk decides to leave weapons with him to help maintain the balance of power on the planet. This was intended as a commentary on the Vietnam War, and was modeled on actual political realities.

"Return to Tomorrow" finds Kirk, Spock, and Dr. Anne Mulhall lending their bodies to the disembodied minds of Sargon, Henoch, and Thalassa, respectively, who are the sole survivors of their advanced civilization. The loan is intended to last just long enough to construct permanent android hosts. Henoch, however, decides to keep Spock's body, and tries to kill Sargon/Kirk, as well as destroy the device holding Spock's displaced mind.

Fortunately, these plans are foiled, and the heroes get their bodies back; the beings decide to enjoy life in the universe without benefit of bodies.

This episode gave Nimoy and Shatner some room to act, and featured the first *Star Trek* appearance of actress Diana Muldaur, as Dr. Mulhall.

"Patterns of Force" features another civilization tampered with by a Federation emissary. In this case it is historian John Gill, who has tried to create an ordered society by using the structure of Nazi Germany. The scheme has backfired, and Gill is drugged and used as a figurehead by Melakon, a very unpleasant fellow. Gill's former history student, James Kirk, and Spock investigate. They're captured, then escape to save yet another addle-brained culture from itself.

"By Any Other Name" concerns alien spies who assume human form only to be confounded by their own newfound human nature. Members of the Kelvan mission to Federation space hijack the *Enterprise* preparatory to the three-hundred-year journey back to their home world. Kirk, Scotty, Spock, and the other crew members not turned into small blocks (!) manage to turn the aliens' passions against them, and the Kelvans give up when they realize that they have become too human to survive on their original planet.

"Omega Glory" features yet another parallel history: the warring Kohms and Yangs parallel the Communists and Yankees of the Vietnam War era. A starship captain has set himself up as warlord with the Kohms; Kirk and Spock finally rally the Yangs when Kirk realizes that their sacred words are actually a distortion of the Preamble to the U.S. Constitution! This powerful episode was written entirely by Roddenberry himself, an unusual occurrence at the time.

Early in 1968, the volume of mail provoked by Bjo Trimble's letter campaign led the network to announce on the air after the March 1, 1968, broadcast of "Omega Glory" that *Star Trek* would, indeed, be returning in the fall.

A press release soon followed:

UNPRECEDENTED VIEWER REACTION IN SUPPORT OF *STAR TREK* LEADS TO ON-AIR ANNOUNCEMENT OF SERIES SCHEDULING FROM 1968-69.

In response to unprecedented viewer reaction in support of the continuation of the NBC Television Network's *Star Trek* series, plans for continuing the series in the Fall were announced on NBC-TV immediately following last Friday night's episode of the space adventure series. The announcement will be repeated following next Friday's program.

From early December to date, NBC has received 114,667 pieces of mail in support of *Star Trek*, and 52,151 in the month of February alone.

Immediately after last Friday night's program, the following announcement was made:

"And now an announcement of interest to all viewers of *Star Trek*. We are pleased to tell you that *Star Trek* will continue to be seen on NBC Television. We know you will be looking forward to seeing the weekly adventure in space on *Star Trek*."

Meanwhile, back on the regular series front, "The Ultimate Computer" is the brainchild, almost literally, of scientist Richard Daystrom, who programs it with his own brain patterns. Installed on the *Enterprise*, the M-5 takes command and decimates the crew of another starship when it mistakes war games for an actual attack. Ultimately Kirk outsmarts the machine and order is restored.

"Bread and Circuses" takes Kirk and crew to a world with a history parallel to that of Earth, with one exception: this world's equivalent of the Roman Empire has lasted well into the twentieth century. (This was undoubtedly very convenient as far as the wardrobe department was concerned.) Captain Merik, a Federation officer, has taken a place of power in this culture, and has gotten rid of his crew by sending them to their deaths in the gladiatorial games.

Kirk, McCoy, and Spock seem faced with a similar fate, but Scotty sabotages the planet's power source, enabling them to escape, and a repentant Merik gives Kirk his communicator before dying. All is well, and as the *Enterprise* leaves they discover that the underground opposition to the "Romans" seems to be a Christian cult, further reinforcing the parallel-history concept.

"Assignment: Earth" incorporated the script of a pilot proposed by Roddenberry into the *Star Trek* continuity. Once again, the *Enterprise* travels through time, this time to 1968. Here they meet Gary Seven (Robert Lansing), a human trained by aliens to defend Earth.

Kirk and Spock follow him to New York. Seven's mission is to prevent the launching of an orbiting defense system that will actually prove disastrous to humanity. Kirk tries to interfere. With the help of Roberta Lincoln (Teri Garr), Seven manages to evade Kirk, but eventually is caught up with; he then manages to convince the captain of the importance of his mission, and the space bomb is destroyed. The story ends with a hint that Seven and Roberta will have more adventures, but a spin-off series never materialized.

Writing in the June 1968 issue of *Variety,* Nimoy stated, "During the first season of *Star Trek* a wise director gave me this advice: 'Build in all the character elements you can find right now while you still have your strength. As time goes on, the attrition will be devastating.' I took his advice and am very grateful for it. The fact is, a great deal of talent is required to work successfully in television—perhaps even more than in features. The finished TV product is nothing more than a series of educated, artistic guesses determined solely by the previous experience of the individuals involved. Time to cogitate, to digest, or to live with an idea before committing it to film is strictly forbidden. The very basic form of creativity is undermined. If you'll forgive a tongue-twisting axiom, 'Thesis versus antithesis results in dramatic synthesis. Time and creative energy provide the dramatic content.' Remove the element of time and the synthesis becomes forced and arbitrary, lacking fresh insight." Nimoy went on to reveal, "On the *Star Trek* set we've actually had rewrites arrive seconds and even minutes after the scene had been shot. Time beats TV by a nose. And the viewers finish out of the money!"

During the between-season break, DeForest Kelley, apparently not the happiest cast member of *Star Trek*, was profiled in *TV Guide* on August 24, 1968.

According to *TV Guide,* Kelley was frustrated that even with two seasons behind him, he wasn't being given the recognition he felt he deserved. "When I see the trade papers, after a whole season, still list only Bill Shatner and Leonard Nimoy as co-stars, I burn a little inside. . . . I've had a rough road in this business, and billing can be an actor's life's blood." Kelley seems to have battled for every privilege, from a studio parking space to a private dressing room.

Billing wasn't Kelley's only beef. "Once I got left out of an episode entirely. I went to the writer—he also has producer status on the show—and he said, very apologetically, 'De, I'm sorry, but it was an oversight.' An oversight! If a writer-producer on my own show forgets me, then I've got a problem!" While Kelley admitted that the nature of their positions on the *Enterprise* gave Shatner and Nimoy more active roles on the show, he was not happy standing silently on the bridge while his colleagues got all the lines.

In spite of Kelley's irritation at this treatment, he was known on the set as easygoing and a perfect "Southern Gentleman," no doubt a result of his Georgia upbringing. He was extremely popular with cast and crew, often going out of his way to remember birthdays and other family events. Leonard Nimoy told *TV Guide,* "De really cares about people." Shatner said, "There's a simple unassuming niceness about this man that's rare in any business."

He probably inherited these traits from his preacher father. Even his dream of acting, he said, probably came from watching his father preach: "A good preacher, like a good lawyer, is a good actor—and my father was a good preacher."

TV Guide showed us the gentler DeForest Kelley, cooking black-eyed peas at New Year's for good luck. And the luck seemed to come in. His wife had clipped and framed his first appearance in a *TV Guide* crossword puzzle. Said Kelley, "It's not an Oscar or an Emmy, but to an actor it's something."

Soon afterward, the Fall Preview of *TV Guide* came out, and had this to say about *Star Trek:*

> More hazardous than all their encounters in outer space for the Star Trekkers are those Nielsen ratings, and they just barely eked by with a renewal for this season. Last term, their future was in considerable doubt, and only a heavy mail campaign from avid viewers played an important part in keeping the show on.
>
> Executive producer Gene Roddenberry still was on the verge of quitting the show because they changed its time slot to 10 P.M. Fridays, a time he

thinks bodes no good for the future of his series, since it slots the show opposite the movies on CBS and *Judd* on ABC. But he did agree to remain with it, despite his unhappiness at the change.

Roddenberry tells us that this season the only change is to expose the secondary characters more fully, to give viewers a better idea of their personalities. He remarks of the gang in *Trek,* "We have the truly multiracial cast, and in two years we've had only three crank letters." In one of the stories this season, the Trekkers land on a planet identical in physical makeup to Earth. On that planet, police are selected as carefully as we select scientists, and the question is posed: Could our police be better? "We are using science fiction to show the police as they could or should be if they had support from the public, and scientific support," explains ex-cop Roddenberry.

This item was, however, more than a bit premature, as Roddenberry did quit. As suspected, NBC was sneakily shifting its stance with regard to *Star Trek*. It had announced that the show would be aired in a 7:30 P.M. prime-time slot on Monday . . . only to turn around and stick *Star Trek* on at 10 P.M. on Friday, a time slot with the stench of certain death. It seemed that *Rowan & Martin's Laugh-In* had a prior claim on that particular time slot. To further compound its infamy, NBC only contracted for thirteen episodes, instead of a full season's worth. (In the end, the series did run a full season one last time.)

Roddenberry planned to put Gene L. Coon in his place, but illness and other commitments kept this from coming about; *Outer Limits* producer Joseph Stefano was invited to step in, but declined. Roddenberry was forced to choose someone untested; although his replacements came highly recommended, they were not familiar with the basic ideas and relationships within the series, and were therefore destined to oversee a number of episodes in which the basic integrity of *Star Trek* and its characters were undermined to varying degrees.

CHAPTER FIVE:

AN AREA OF TURBULENCE

(THE THIRD AND FINAL SEASON)

ome years later, DeForest Kelley would reflect on the series' final season. "The third year was not a good year because there was too much going on: problems with the network, thinking we were going to be dropped, bad time slots. A kind of internal revolution took place, so to speak, and it began to show, which we were all very concerned about.

"[Gene Roddenberry] began to slack off in the latter part of the second season because other things entered into what then was thought to be a successful show. Demands began to be put upon his time in other directions and he then, in turn, brought in other people to assist him. The third year he began to battle with NBC over the time slot and he became terribly upset and told them he would not produce the show personally if it were placed in a ten o'clock time slot on Friday night. We had a tremendous university audience and school audience and it would lose viewers if it were on at that time. NBC went ahead and did it and Gene pulled out. They brought another producer in who was not familiar with the show and it began to go downhill."

Indeed, on September 20, 1968, *Star Trek* began its third and final season with what may rightly be considered its single worst episode: "Spock's Brain."

In "Spock's Brain," the object in question is stolen by a beautiful woman who then vanishes. McCoy manages to keep Spock's body going, and they take it with them when they reach the woman's planet. It seems that the brain is needed to run the planet's power system. This computer even speaks with Spock's voice. Eventually the brain is regained, and McCoy uses an alien teaching device to provide him, temporarily, with the knowledge necessary to return Spock's brain to his body.

"The *Enterprise* Incident" sends the *Enterprise* on what is essentially an espionage mission: Kirk feigns a mental breakdown and takes the ship into the Neutral Zone. Outgunned by Romulans, he is captured, and Spock denounces his actions. McCoy beams to the Romulan ship just as Kirk attacks Spock; Spock kills the captain with the Vulcan death grip and the body is beamed back to the *Enterprise*. Of course, there is no Vulcan death grip, and Kirk is revived, surgically altered to look like a Romulan, and beamed back to steal the Romulan cloaking device. The *Enterprise* makes good its escape once Scotty gets the stolen cloaking device installed and working.

Fans, however, were highly critical of the episode for the way Spock acted out of character; D. C. Fontana bore the brunt of the blame for this for a time, until it was revealed that her original story had been rewritten by other hands.

"The Paradise Syndrome" strands an amnesiac Kirk on a planet while the *Enterprise* must seek and destroy an asteroid headed directly for that world. The attempt fails and the damaged ship heads back at sublight speed. In the months that this takes, Kirk is hailed as a god by the Native American-like natives of the planet. He falls in love with a priestess and marries her.

Meanwhile, Spock deciphers the inscriptions on an obelisk near Kirk's home and discovers that it is a device to deflect asteroids. Kirk and his wife are supposed to know how to activate it; when they can't, the people stone them. Spock arrives just in time to set off the device, saving the planet, but Kirk's pregnant wife dies from her injuries.

"And the Children Shall Lead" involves the children on a scientific outpost. All the children's parents committed suicide and the kids are under the influence of "the friendly angel" Gorgan, in truth an evil entity. The ship is threatened but Gorgan's aims are thwarted when the children remember their parents and turn against him.

"Is There in Truth No Beauty?" is the question posed when a Medusan comes on board; this race cannot be looked upon by humanoid eyes. Kollos, who stays in a protective case, is accompanied by the telepathic Dr. Miranda Jones. Marvick, an engineer on board, has been in love with Jones for years, and is driven by jealousy to try to kill Kollos.

The sight of the alien drives him mad, and he goes, crazed, to engineering and casts the ship into strange uncharted regions of space. The Medusan's amazing navigational powers are the only hope; Spock performs a mind meld wearing protective eyeglasses, but forgets them and is driven mad, too, after the ship is saved. Jones, who is revealed to be blind, must overcome her own attachment to Kollos in order to help Spock.

This marks the second *Star Trek* appearance of Diana Muldaur, who plays Dr. Miranda Jones.

"Spectre of the Gun" hurls Kirk and crew into a deadly simulation of the gunfight at the O.K. Corral. Only by accepting it as an illusion can they survive. But only by refusing to kill can they prove to the Melkotians, who put them there, that they deserve their place in the universe.

"The Day of the Dove" pits the Federation crew against Klingons, all at the machinations of a being that feeds off hostile and violent emotions. When the Klingons are captured and taken on board, the alien turns phasers into swords, and battles ensue. The wounded are healed to fight again. Kirk eventually convinces the Klingon commander, Kang, that they must work together, and they put on a convincing show of friendship that drives the evil being away.

"For the World Is Hollow and I Have Touched the Sky" concerns the world of Yonada. The people there are controlled by the Oracle and don't realize that their planet is actually a space ship. Yonada is headed for a disastrous collision with a giant asteroid. A landing crew beams down, including Dr. McCoy, who has learned that he has an incurable terminal disease. He falls in love with the high priestess and is prepared to stay with her. Kirk and Spock manage to reach the Oracle computer's memory banks, and obtain information that will save Yonada . . . and cure McCoy, who bids a wistful farewell to his new flame.

In "The Tholian Web," the *Enterprise* discovers a dead ship that seems to be drifting into another dimension. When the rest of the survey crew returns, Kirk is stranded on the ship when it disappears. His air supply is limited, and rescue efforts are hindered by the fact that the area of space causes humans to act aggressively toward each other. Kirk's ghostly figure, caught in an interdimensional limbo, begins appearing to the crew at intervals. The Tholians, an unknown race, show up, accuse the Federation of trespassing, and begin to spin the web of the title. Spock eludes them, and Kirk is rescued just in the nick of time.

"Plato's Stepchildren" are the inhabitants of Platonius, who have great telekinetic powers but no immunity to disease. When McCoy beams down to help them, he, along with Kirk and Spock, is subjected to their cruel whims. Nurse Chapel and Uhura are drawn into these humiliations; Spock is forced to sing. Alexander, a powerless dwarf, tries to help them but cannot. Finally, McCoy figures out that the powers of the Platonians derive from a chemical in their systems. With this knowledge, he is able to duplicate those powers for himself and his fellow crewmen. They escape, and free Alexander from his malicious masters. This episode is notable for having featured television's first interracial kiss, as Kirk and Uhura are forced to kiss by the malicious superbeings.

"Wink of an Eye" describes the condition of the Scalosians, whose radioactive water has sped up their liferate so fast that they can only be perceived as a buzzing noise. When Kirk takes some of this water, he can perceive them, but his crew cannot sense him. The Scalosians plan to use him to repopulate their world. McCoy devises an antidote but Spock must first take some water and be sped up himself in order to find and save the captain.

"The Empath" is Gem, a beautiful mute woman. Kirk and McCoy are kidnapped and tortured by aliens; Gem is an empath who can absorb their pain and injuries, healing the terrible agonies inflicted on them. McCoy's injuries threaten to kill him, but she prevents this, risking her own life. This cruel test turns out to have a humane motivation, of sorts: two planets are threatened by an imminent disaster, but the aliens can only save the inhabitants of one, and have been trying to determine which race is more worthy of survival.

"Elaan of Troyius" is on the *Enterprise* on her way to a diplomatically advantageous marriage, but she's more interested in Kirk; when she cries, the touch of her tears chemically induces Kirk to fall in love with her. Klingons confound matters, but all works out when Elaan's jewels turn out to be dilithium crystals. Kirk ultimately breaks free of her spell and she proceeds with her important mission.

"Whom Gods Destroy" takes place on a planetary asylum for the last group of mentally ill people in human society. Kirk brings a new drug that can cure these last vestiges of madness, but the asylum has been taken over by a shape-changing madman, who tries to steal the *Enterprise* by taking Kirk's form. The astute Mr. Spock manages to determine which is the real Jim and saves the day.

"Let That Be Your Last Battlefield" tackles prejudice by reducing it to absurdity. Lokai, late of the planet Cheron, is half black and half white, being neatly bisected, pigmentwise, right down the middle. When he shows up on the *Enterprise*, he is pursued by Bele, who looks exactly the same . . . except that his coloration makes him a mirror image of Lokai. This left/right distinction has been the root of hatred on their home world for generations. When the *Enterprise* finally reaches Cheron, after nearly being demolished by the battles between the two passengers, it is revealed to be completely dead. Lokai and Bele beam down to their world to continue their ancient, pointless conflict to their deaths.

In "The Mark of Gideon," Kirk seems to disappear while beaming down . . . at least from the perspective of the bridge. Kirk, on the other hand, finds himself on the bridge completely alone, with no trace of Spock or the others. This is in fact an exact replica of the real *Enterprise*. Kirk has been kidnapped because the people of Gideon, free from all disease, are suffering from overpopulation. Kirk, having survived one deadly disease, still carries it, and the plan is to use him to introduce disease back into the world of Gideon. Spock manages to find and rescue him, but not before this new vector has been unleashed on Gideon.

"That Which Survives" is the holographic image of a beautiful woman; the projection's touch is fatal. Designed to keep other races away from the artifacts of a long-dead civilization, she costs several lives, and nearly gets Mr. Sulu before Spock manages to pull the plug on the ancient computer.

"The Lights of Zetar" are the disembodied survivors of Zetar, who seek a host in which to continue their existence. They settle on Lt. Mira Romaine, an officer supervising the transfer of the Federation's records to a new library facility. They possess her, which seriously hampers the possibility of romance between her and Scotty. The Lights are finally driven out when Mira enters a pressure chamber.

To write this episode, Jeremy Tarcher teamed up with Shari Lewis, the puppeteer famous for her sidekick Lamb Chop.

"Requiem for Methuselah" takes Kirk and crew to Holberg 917G in search of the antidote to a deadly disease. There they encounter a Mr. Flint and Reena, a beautiful young lady, and Kirk falls for her right off the bat. Eventually it is discovered that Flint is actually an immortal who lived on Earth for centuries; among his aliases were da Vinci and Brahms. But without Earth's atmosphere to preserve him, his immortality is nearing its end. Reena is the last of a series of androids he has constructed to keep him company. This bothers Kirk more than a bit, so Spock obligingly clears Kirk's mind of the unhappy memory.

"The Way to Eden" is sought by the charismatic but crazed Dr. Sevrin and his youthful disciples, who could only be described as space hippies. One of them is an old flame of Chekov's, and he tries to understand her new interests but just can't get the swing of it.

Kirk must give the seekers free rein of his ship, due to the presence of an important diplomat's son among them. Ultimately, Sevrin incapacitates the bridge crew and steals a shuttle.

He and his followers find Eden, a truly beautiful planet, but everything about it is toxic. Sevrin and one young man die before the others can be rescued. The original version of this script included Dr. McCoy's daughter Joanna among the young seekers, but she was dropped, and in fact never appeared in the series despite several planned attempts to feature her as a character.

"The Cloud Minders" dwell in the skyborne city of Stratos; the Troglytes live on the surface of Ardana, excavating zenite for the benefit of their social superiors. When Kirk arrives seeking zenite, needed to resolve a crisis on another world, he cannot avoid getting entangled in this inequitable situation.

He eventually resolves the situation by intentionally trapping himself and leaders of both classes in a mine shaft, where the Troglytes' alleged inferiority and brutality are demonstrated to be merely an effect of gases in the mines. Kirk leaves with the zenite, sure in the knowledge that social reforms are finally under way.

In "The Savage Curtain," the *Enterprise* is hailed by Abraham Lincoln, who just happens to be floating in space nearby. Kirk and Spock follow the dead president to the lava-ridden surface of a nearby planet. Yarnek, a stone creature desirous of understanding the concepts of "good" and "evil," pits them, along with Vulcan philosopher Surak, against Genghis Khan, a notorious Klingon, a killer from Earth's past, and a famous bloodthirsty criminal. A philosophical slugfest, where the main question is: if Yarnek doesn't know good from evil . . . how does he know who to put on which side?!?

"All Our Yesterdays" involves another time portal through which Kirk, Spock, and McCoy pass. This one is located on the planet Sarpeidon, whose people have fled an impending nova by relocating to various different periods in their past history. Kirk goes through first and winds up in an era similar to Reformation England, where he is in danger of being killed as a witch.

Spock and the doctor find themselves in a prehistoric ice age, where the Vulcan reverts to his ancestors' lustful ways and becomes involved with a woman, Zarabeth. They believe that they cannot return to their temporal starting point without dying, but this is not actually true, as they did not undergo the necessary treatments. Meanwhile, Kirk resolves his troubles with the help of another time traveler, and manages to reclaim his friends and get back to the ship just before the nova destroys the planet.

"Turnabout Intruder," the final *Star Trek* episode to be filmed, was dubbed "Captain Kirk, Space Queen" by the crew. Here, a woman once spurned by Kirk in favor of his Starfleet career gets her revenge by switching bodies with him and taking over his ship! Spock determines the truth of this by using a Vulcan mind meld on Dr. Janice Lester's body, but has a hard time convincing anyone that Kirk's body is occupied by a woman.

Spock brings McCoy into a plan to rescue Kirk, but the two are discovered and sentenced to death for mutiny. Fortunately, the rest of the ship begins to realize that something is drastically amiss, and Kirk himself shakes off the effects of the mind transfer.

A rather intriguing acting chore, this role was apparently enlivened by William Shatner's off-camera gags. In one scene, when McCoy examines Kirk, Shatner slipped off a hospital robe to reveal plastic breasts. Unperturbed, DeForest Kelley stayed in character, leading Shatner to break up into hysterical laughter. Needless to say, this never made it into the final cut. Shatner, perhaps obsessed with the theme of this episode, at one point appeared on set in full drag. Later in the shooting, Shatner came down with a vicious case of the flu, but still kept up his shooting schedule.

Final word of *Star Trek*'s cancellation came through during this shooting; when "Turnabout Intruder" wrapped, it was a wrap for *Star Trek* as well. If the network had gone ahead with filming the last few completed scripts, Shatner would have made his debut as director in the very next episode.

"Turnabout Intruder" was also the last *Star Trek* episode to be aired; it was broadcast on June 3, 1969. In August, when the final network rerun aired, it was "Requiem for Methuselah" and the last word spoken was by Spock, who said, "Forget. . . ."

But many would not.

CHAPTER SIX:

MOVING THROUGH LIMBO AND BEYOND

(THE LOST YEARS . . . TO *STAR TREK: THE MOTION PICTURE*)

lthough to the casual observer it might have seemed that Gene Roddenberry's brainchild was dead and buried, this was not the case. The seventies were actually the decade when national interest in *Star Trek* began to build at an incredible rate. Already having a strong base of support, it could only draw more fans than ever as the series began to repeat again and again in syndication. As early as 1972, *TV Guide* made note of this:

> All over the country, people are wearing "*Star Trek* Lives" T-shirts, pasting Mr. Spock bumpers on their cars, and maybe, for all I know, falling on their knees before graven images of Mr. Spock.

The cause of this fanatic fandom was the first-ever *Star Trek* convention, held in January of 1972, almost three years after the show's cancellation.

At the convention, the *TV Guide* reporter spoke with Shirley Gerstel of Paramount Television.

> "The calls and letters that come into my office are tremendous. I keep passing them on to the West Coast. I never thought that *Star Trek* would come back, but now there's a rumor that Paramount might start making it again."

This was indeed the biggest buzz at the convention, with Trekkies dreaming of the possibility between screenings of the thirteen old episodes Paramount had provided. Gene Roddenberry, guest of honor at the convention, wasn't yet convinced, but the convention was starting to work its magic. Said Roddenberry,

> "I didn't think it was possible six months ago, but after seeing the enthusiasm here, I'm beginning to change my mind. We had such a family group on the show that it's totally different for us. We still meet and drink together, and we're still all friends, so for this show it is possible."

In 1973, *Star Trek* finally returned to the airwaves . . . as a Saturday morning animated series. Although Leonard Nimoy seemed less than enthusiastic about the idea, he signed on to provide Spock's voice. Interviewed by the *L.A. Free Press* before work on the cartoon had actually begun, he sighed when asked about it; he wasn't certain that the new series wouldn't reduce *Star Trek* to an idiotic piece of juvenilia:

> "That's why I sigh. We don't know. Unfortunately, I don't have control over the material. I will have control only to the extent that I can refuse to do a script that is sent to me, and then I am in breach of

contract, and we start with that whole business again.

"I was in Florida when this thing came up and I was contacted by mail and by phone. It was very difficult. All the people who were doing it were here in California, and I was assured by all—my agent and Gene Roddenberry and Dorothy Fontana, who's going to produce the show—that the intention was to do a very special kind of animation, to really use the medium properly and successfully and to maintain the quality that *Star Trek* originally was intended to have. And, that the material would be new, fresh, good stuff. We were really going to do it right.

"Okay. Everybody starts out with good intentions. I have never met a producer or a writer who came to me and said, 'We are going to do something that is going to be so lousy . . .' Nobody ever says that. I believe that these people mean it. But when the exigencies set in, they start to turn out some scripts. They take them to [the] people who are financing it and they say, 'Oh, wait a minute, we can't do this, I mean, this script would be terrific for a philosophy department at UCLA, but not for a Saturday morning cartoon television. It won't work.'

"Then the arguments start. And it's a question of how tough they're going to be and how strong they're going to be in taking a stand on what is good *Star Trek*."

The rest of the cast reprised their roles as well, with the exception of Walter Koenig, who kept his hand in with a script. Two new alien characters were added; James Doohan and Majel Barrett did extra duty, providing the voices for the new characters as well as most of the supporting cast as well.

DeForest Kelley (in the Gulick interview) noted that Roddenberry's involvement with the animated series faded somewhat after a strong beginning:

"Dorothy Fontana was really running that show. Because it is so dependent on artists, there was not much Gene could do except see to it that above-average scripts were sent in for it. And you'll notice that most of the scripts were not written for children. They are adult scripts and some of them are very good, and would have made good [live-action] *Star Trek*s.

"I did two animated shows here in Lubbock [Texas, where Kelley was appearing in the play *Beginner's Luck* at the time of this interview] a couple of weeks ago. To do those two scripts took me a little over an hour, because I gave four or five readings of each line. In case they didn't like the way I read a line, I'd read it three or four more times, so they could pick the one they wanted. It was a little bit time-consuming."

At the time, there was some thought that the animated series might serve as the first in the necessary series of events needed to get a live-action *Star Trek* back on the air in prime time. Again, DeForest Kelley:

"That was Gene's thought, I think. I questioned it at the time he said he was going to do it, as I thought it was the death blow. Gene said, 'No, I don't feel that way at all. I think it's important to keep some form of *Star Trek* alive and in the minds of people.'

"It's not the network," Kelley pointed out, that was keeping the series from being revived. "The network wants the show again and would love to have it back. But Paramount, the studio which owns *Star Trek*, doesn't want to make *Star Trek* prime time because they're making so much money in syndication with it. They feel they would be competing with themselves."

As far as a "real" *Star Trek* revival went, Kelley was ready and willing to dust off Dr. McCoy's medical diploma and medical tools.

"I would go with it if everybody else went with it. I think if the whole cast was pulled together again it would be nice.

"It was a very satisfying show to do because it was such a loved show.

"I think we all feel that way. But we now know the tremendous impact that it has made and is still making. It is rather a delight to be associated with it, even though it's been a mixed blessing for me. I think it's hurt my career. I didn't realize that until the last couple of years. I found myself so identified with it, and the identification has grown stronger over the years. If *Star Trek* doesn't renew itself, it is my job to break that identification and get back into what I was doing, or something else.

"I believe the popularity of *Star Trek* is stronger than it has ever been. It will, in my opinion, be very difficult to ever have another show that has created the kind of feeling that *Star Trek* has created. I doubt very seriously if there will ever be another one. It was a one-of-a-kind thing."

The idea for the animated series was pitched to Gene Roddenberry by Lou Scheimer and Norm Prescott of Filmation, one of the higher-quality television animation studios; although not fully animated, their productions had more movement than the average Saturday morning fodder.

Roddenberry was swayed by their intention to honor the show's dignity and its original ideals; no cute kids or anthropomorphic canines would be added to the *Enterprise* crew. Scripts were provided by numerous *Star Trek* alumni: David Gerrold (author of "The Trouble with Tribbles"), Samuel Peeples (who wrote the second *Star Trek* pilot), and Marc Daniels (who directed thirteen episodes of the original series) were all contributing writers.

Unfortunately, despite its noble intentions, the animated *Star Trek* came across generally stiff and lifeless. The animation was partly at fault here, as the new characters were merely visual representations with no real personalities. Some of the writing, such as Walter Koenig's "The Infinite Vulcan" script (which involved giant Spock clones!), left a great deal to be desired.

Rehashes of bizarre aging diseases and tribbles (this time they grew to immense size)—did little to make the project a fountainhead of originality. The fact that the cast recorded their parts at different locations around the country did little to help re-create the original feeling of camaraderie of the original series, and in fact the actors often came across as though they were merely reciting lines rather than interacting with their fellow cast members.

One of the animated *Star Trek*'s twenty-two episodes, however, is worthy of some further comment: "Yesteryear," by D. C. Fontana. This story, featuring the Guardian of Forever from "The City on the Edge of Forever" (voiced by James Doohan, who worked overtime on this series), involves Spock's journey through time back to his childhood on Vulcan, which has somehow caused a sort of time distortion.

He encounters himself at the point during his youth when he was torn between his human and Vulcan heritages; the dramatic focus of the story is the death of his pet sehlat, I-Chaya (mentioned in "Journey to Babel").

The network (again, NBC) wanted a happy ending, as the death of a pet, they feared, would upset young viewers, but Fontana fought for her original drama and won. She expressed her feelings on this issue a year later in a fanzine article:

"I-Chaya's death was absolutely necessary to the story. Part of Spock's training had to do with the facing of responsibilities and realities. One of the greatest weaknesses of children's programming on television, especially animation, is the presentation of total nonreality. Things do die—plants, pets, and people. Is there anyone who, as a child, has not suffered the loss of a pup? In deciding that I-Chaya should die with peace and dignity rather than pain and suffering, young Spock accepted reality and responsibility."

In reality, D. C. Fontana's thoughtful and sensitive script was her only contribution to the animated *Star Trek,* and the series soon faded out and away. Interestingly, Alan Dean Foster, the noted science fiction author, wrote a *Star Trek Log* series of paperbacks that served much the same purposes for the cartoon series as the late James Blish's prose adaptations did for the original show; Foster wove the stories together in each volume, often adding to them the depth that was sadly missing from the episodes themselves. The animated *Star Trek* ran during the 1973 and 1974 television seasons; the episodes are now available on home videocassettes.

Another indication of *Star Trek*'s undying popularity came to light on September 19, 1974, *Star Trek* Day at the Movieland Wax Museum in Buena Park, California. Unveiled to the public that day, in response to the frequent requests found in the museum's suggestion box, was a replica of the U.S.S. *Enterprise* bridge, occupied by lifelike wax representations of Kirk, Spock, McCoy, and Uhura. (Scotty, Sulu, and Chekov would be added to the display in 1978.)

Sculpted by Lia de Lio and detailed by Logan Fleming, these uncannily realistic figures made quite an impression on their real-life counterparts, who were in attendance at the gala opening: William Shatner, Nichelle Nichols, DeForest Kelley, and Leonard Nimoy. Also in attendance were Gene Roddenberry and wife Majel Barrett, who was not represented in the display.

In 1975, *The Tomorrow Show,* hosted by Tom Snyder, featured guests DeForest Kelley, James Doohan, Walter Koenig, and Harlan Ellison. They discussed the enduring popularity of *Star Trek* and the rumors of a revival as a feature film. It was a very windy hour, but among the more interesting comments were those of Walter Koenig, who commented:

> "The only problem is, if [*Star Trek*] is a feature film as opposed to a made-for-television show, they'll decide that they have to change the thrust of it in some way, make it monsters and huge battle scenes; something that you can't get on television. You may distort the entire feeling of the show."

Time would prove Koenig to be absolutely correct.

Finally, in 1975, Paramount Pictures announced its intention to provide a budget of two to three million dollars for a *Star Trek* film, if Roddenberry could provide a script that suited them. His initial submission, in which the *Enterprise* and its crew met God (or an entity calling itself God, a fine semantical and theological distinction, as Philip K. Dick once observed), seemed a bit too outre for the studio, so it began to look at scripts from other sources.

John D. F. Black submitted an outline, as did Theodore Sturgeon, Robert Silverberg, and even Ray Bradbury. Harlan Ellison's encounter with a dimwitted producer who insisted that Ellison's proposed story would be acceptable only if it was reworked to include ancient Mayans (the man had been reading Von Daniken, it seems) is legendary.

In the midst of this constant hunt for a marketable script, DeForest Kelley commented, rather dryly that what Paramount was really looking for was "*Jaws* in space."

Also in 1975, Leonard Nimoy released an autobiographical book with what was, to some *Star Trek* aficionados, an ominous (if not downright sinister) title, *I Am Not Spock*.

The book was in fact a well-balanced look at an actor's life and career, examining Nimoy's work and focusing on his relationship with the character that made him famous. In some humorous passages, Nimoy actually engages in imaginary conversations with Spock on a variety of subjects; at some points the similarities between the two personas outnumbered the differences.

Basically, the book gets across the fact that Nimoy existed independently of, and in fact before, the character with whom he is associated. It does not demean the character or *Star Trek* in any way.

In fact, it celebrates the possibilities that *Star Trek* introduced into Nimoy's life after nearly two decades of struggle for work and recognition. The cover features a shadowy photograph of Nimoy, still wearing his Spock haircut and giving the Vulcan salute; the ears are obscured, leaving their actual contours to the viewer's imagination.

The cover was also available from the publisher (Celestial Arts) as a poster bearing the greeting "Live long and prosper." This was certainly not the work of a man who hated the role he'd been playing.

And yet some fans, whose lives seemed to hinge on a *Star Trek* revival, chose to view Nimoy's choice of title as an affront, and an indication that he was cruelly planning to deprive them of their favorite entertainment—if entertainment is an adequate word to describe what their sometimes mindless devotion to the series provided them with.

If this seems an unfair description of some *Star Trek* fans, bear in mind that it only describes an extreme fringe element, and consider this excerpt from a letter received by Leonard Nimoy some time after the publication of *I Am Not Spock:*

"Good for you. Do not return to *Star Trek.* I approve your pretensions to stardom. I look forward to your wrecking the greatest show of all time with your ******* tactics. Big man, big money, big book. *I Am Not Spock.* Really fantastic. We all will cheer when you and your fellow star William Shatner gut the *Enterprise* of her captain and executive officer.

"Why the hell should the ******* series go on now if you're going to kick it in the groin before production starts? You and your 'career' can take two running steps straight into hell. We made you and we will unmake you. So you're not Spock, huh? The one, the only slimy character of the Sixties to be put in the Hall of Fame of video along with Matt Dillon and Lucy Ricardo when everything else about television is lost to memory fifty years ago, the one bloody character that became an icon to a generation. I got news for you, as long as you live, you will only be known as Spock, Vulcan hero to a planet of youth. I hereby put a curse on your miserable future career. May 100 million hands turn dials when you appear on the TV screen."

If this bellicose and confused correspondence seems a unique case, consider that renowned writer Harlan Ellison once had one of his public speaking engagements disrupted by a young woman who took exception to his assertion that he had written the words spoken by Spock in "The City on the Edge of Forever." Bursting into hysterics, she was appalled that anyone could say such horrible things, as to her Spock was terribly real, and not a fictional creation of other minds.

Fortunately, the bulk of *Star Trek* fans are well-balanced individuals attracted by Roddenberry's message of a hopeful, positive future, in many cases highly trained professional people, and not the handful of unrepresentative, deranged basket cases that have just been discussed.

In a 1976 wire service interview, Roddenberry candidly revealed his own constant surprise at the widespread fervor surrounding his famous creation:

"Sometimes I wish I could walk out the door and leave *Star Trek* behind," says Gene Roddenberry, the man who created the television series and steered it through 79 episodes.

It is not that he has any less affection for his creation. He simply worries that the Starship *Enterprise* and its voyagers will take over his life. "I'm not a guru and I don't want to be" he says. "It frightens me when I learn of ten thousand people treating a *Star Trek* script as if it were scripture.

"As to the *Star Trek* conventions: I have to limit myself to one in the East and one in the West each year. I'm not a performer and frankly those conventions scare the hell out of me.

"It is scary to be surrounded by a thousand people asking questions as if the events in the series actually happened. I'm just afraid that if it goes too far and it appears that I have created a philosophy that answers all human ills that someone will stand up and cry 'Fraud!' And with good reason.

"I expect that if the feature turns out well, Paramount will try to bring *Star Trek* back to television. I would hope that it would take the form of occasional films in the long form. I don't think I could face the insanity of another weekly *Star Trek*."

Eventually, Paramount pulled the plug on the feature film idea, and *Star Trek* fell back into its all-too-familiar limbo.

In an August 1977 interview, William Shatner expressed his feelings on this latest setback (this is one commentary not likely to appear in any of Paramount's official *Star Trek* histories):

"I feel that it was an idiotic decision by the people at Paramount. A *Star Trek* feature would be both an entertainment and financial success, and its blockage stands as one of the greatest monuments to stupidity.

"As far as I know the movie has been finally canceled and, in the light of the success of *Star Wars,* I just can't understand it."

In fact, the surprise success of *Star Wars* may very well have *been* the reason for the turnaround. Paramount couldn't see the success of George Lucas's film as anything other than an unduplicatable, one-shot fluke.

Later in 1977, plans were finally launched for a proposed new series, to be entitled *Star Trek II.* Apparently, now Paramount envisioned itself as the force behind a "fourth network," a preposterous-enough-seeming idea at the time which did not come to fruition until January

1995, when Paramount launched its new network UPN, with *Star Trek: Voyager.*

Roddenberry pulled a treatment out of his files entitled "Robot's Return," which had been intended for his series *Genesis II,* which never made it beyond the pilot stage (CBS went for the *Planet of the Apes* TV series instead). This story involved the return of an ancient satellite to Earth, a satellite which has gained sentience and seeks its creator, a being called NASA. This, strongly reminiscent of Nomad in "The Changeling," would be the focus of *Star Trek II*'s first episode.

Roddenberry gave the treatment to Alan Dean Foster, who turned it into a *Star Trek* story, with one notable difference: instead of Spock, the science officer on the *Enterprise* bridge is one Lieutenant Xon (known briefly and rather generically as Lieutenant Vulcan), as Leonard Nimoy seemed quite possibly to be unavailable for his role as Spock. The remaining principals had signed; in fact, Nimoy had no problems with returning to the role of Spock, but was holding out in order to resolve his long-standing royalties dispute with Paramount Pictures.

They had made millions of dollars from merchandise—toys, lunch boxes, books, and the like—which bore his likeness, and he had not received so much as a single penny from all these revenues.

Meanwhile, actor David Gautreaux was cast as Xon, and Persis Khambatta was signed to play a new character, the exotic and alluring (not to mention hairless) Ilia. A third character, Commodore Decker, was not cast.

Writing proceeded apace, and the "Robot's Return" treatment was developed into a script, "In Thy Image," by Harold Livingston and Robert Goodwin. Other scripts were also written: "Kitumba," by John Meredyth Lucas; "Deadlock," by David Ambrose; "Tomorrow and the Stars" by Larry Alexander; "The Savage Syndrome," by Margaret Armen and Alf Harris; "The Child," by John

Povill and Jaron Summers; "Home," by Worley Thorne; "Home," by Theodore Sturgeon; and "Devil's Due," by Bill Lansford.

As preproduction for *Star Trek II* continued, plans also developed to make the pilot film something special that could be marketed as a theatrical release in Europe.

Things then began to pick up. The fourth-network idea looked like a potential washout, so Paramount decided to go full-bore and convert the television project into a theatrical release. Furthermore, the success of Steven Spielberg's *Close Encounters of the Third Kind* seemed a solid enough refutation of their initial view of *Star Wars* as a fluke; obviously, the public would spend its hard-earned money to attend science fiction films. The bottom line, as always, was cold, hard cash.

The director of *Star Trek: The Motion Picture* was to be Robert Wise, director of the classic *The Day the Earth Stood Still,* which had starred Michael Rennie and Patricia Neal.

Anticipation was great; rumors that Kirk and the crew met God still persisted from some years earlier, but were disproven by the final product itself.

The movie scriptwriters began with the old episode "Robot's Return" and used it to develop the full-length feature.

In the opening sequence, three Klingon cruisers are destroyed by a new and unknown alien force that proves resistant to all attacks. A Federation space station warns Earth that the object is headed directly for the planet. *Admiral* Kirk, now on Earth, has been briefed on the new threat, and will take a new *Enterprise* on her maiden voyage in the planet's defense.

Joined by Mr. Scott in dry dock, Kirk can't beam directly to the ship, but must take a shuttle pod, thereby getting a spectacular view of the new ship. The original *Enterprise* crew have received promotions, and await

Kirk. Also on the bridge is Captain Decker, who reluctantly yields his command to Kirk. The crew is complete when a mysterious shuttlecraft brings an unusually cold and aloof Spock to the *Enterprise*. Failing to achieve the Vulcan ritual of Kohlinar, Spock joins the mission because he believes that an encounter with the alien's perfect logic will cleanse him of his human emotions.

The adventure really begins when the alien object attacks the *Enterprise*. Spock discovers that it is trying to communicate and establishes a mental link. The attack ceases, but Lieutenant Ilia disappears from the bridge and is returned, transformed into an alien probe created to communicate with and learn about the humans. She tells the crew that the entity is called "Vejur," or V'Ger.

Kirk discovers that the entity is *Voyager* VI, a twentieth-century space probe, now a sentient being. When V'Ger cannot be diverted from its attack, Captain Decker volunteers to merge with the probe and redirect it. Together with the craft, Decker and Ilia ascend to a higher level of being. Spock learns to embrace his humanity, and renews his friendship with Kirk.

With Earth rescued, the crew on board, and a beautiful new *Enterprise*, *Star Trek* picks up where it left off— boldly going where no man has gone before.

The problem with this movie was its slow, ponderous development, its all-too awestruck reverence for its own special effects (which are beautifully done—but frequently all too static), and most of all the short shrift it gives to its characters' relationships with each other. In essence, the film is too clinical and dispassionate to engage the emotions.

In scenes cut from the theatrical release but restored on video, this is somewhat less the case; each character has his moments. Here, Spock actually weeps after his mind meld with V'Ger. Why these scenes were cut remains a mystery. Another restored scene, showing a space-suited

Kirk emerging from a cargo bay, is notable for the fact that no special effects were ever cued into it; the viewer can see, briefly, the soundstage structure behind him.

Leonard Nimoy had this to say about *Star Trek: The Motion Picture:*

> "I think we should say, in deference to the people who made the first *Star Trek* motion picture, that they had a very special set of problems. For example, there had not been a *Star Trek* project for eleven years. We finished making the series in 1968 and here we were in 1979, coming together to do a different *Star Trek* project. That meant that a lot of very special circumstances had to be addressed. Ground had to be broken in a special kind of way. Do you make comment in the film that eleven years has passed and therefore things have changed? The ship has changed, the uniform has changed, the sets have changed, rank has changed, relationships have changed. We were faced with the concern that we should not be perceived as a blown-up television episode, but should be looked upon as a motion picture. Therefore there were certain changes that were expected by the audience, and they must be addressed."

However one looks at it, the final result was a bit pallid. An alternative ending, devised by Douglas Trumbull's cohort Mike Minor, was rejected as too costly; the film had already gone way over budget to make its December 7, 1979, release date.

One Paramount executive dubbed the production a "thirty-five-million-dollar turkey," but cost estimates actually may make that figure another ten million higher; the film grossed one hundred and five million dollars in the United States. The scuttled ending featured the

Enterprise being ejected from V'Ger, followed by the three Klingon ships from the start of the movie; a battle royale was to ensue, in which the triumphant but damaged *Enterprise* was to be obliged to undergo a saucer separation—an idea that would eventually turn up elsewhere.

Supposedly, director Robert Wise was unhappy with the final cut of the film; Paramount vetoed any reediting in order to make the all-important release date. People who attended the Washington, D.C., premiere of the feature reported observing Wise burying his face in his hands at various points in the film, obviously embarrassed.

Roddenberry's novelization of the script contains just the sort of background information and human interest that the film sorely needed.

Kirk, it seems, was semiretired, involved with a woman who was also using him as a public relations figurehead for Starfleet; based in San Francisco, he spent his off years lecturing extensively about his space adventures. The person who dies in the early transporter accident with Commander Sonak was actually the woman in Kirk's life, a detail left out of the film.

Also in the novel: Ilia's potent sexual chemistry has a clear effect on Sulu, as he becomes physically aroused in her presence. Again, the scene reveals a lot about both characters, but never made it to the screen, not even in the video restoration. So, although the video release provides the opportunity to see *Star Trek: The Motion Picture* at its best, the film remains a fairly disappointing first contact with the big screen as far as the *Star Trek* mythos is concerned.

CHAPTER SEVEN:

SAILING THE
SILVER SCREEN

(THE MOVIE
TRILOGY)

I n 1982, the second *Star Trek* feature, *Star Trek II: The Wrath of Khan,* redressed the failing of its predecessor. It contains a strong, engaging plot, plenty of action, a powerful nemesis, dramatic relationships, a famous controversy—and a notorious continuity glitch.

Early in 1980, Leonard Nimoy, while promoting his television movie *Seizure: The Kathy Morris Story,* in which he played a neurosurgeon involved in a serious brain surgery case, had a few thoughts on *Star Trek* and its future, as reported in this AP wire service story dated January 1, 1980:

Nimoy was just back from New York and Washington, where he had attended the premiere of *Star Trek* and promoted the movie on NBC's *Today* show.

Asked if he had signed yet for a *Star Trek* sequel,

Nimoy, who starred in the television series of the same name, said, "There is nothing definite yet, but I gather there's a lot of conversation at Paramount about what to do with *Star Trek* next."

He said he does want to make something clear. "Some people have a conception that I have trouble playing other characters, that I'm too identified with Spock. It's no problem. It would probably be more dramatic to say it is.

"When I work in the theater, I can feel it in the first few minutes on stage. Particularly from people who have seen me in *Star Trek*. They're trying to focus on Spock and what I'm going to be doing.

"When I played Sherlock Holmes, he was a character very close to Spock because of his logical deductions. But there was no problem."

But despite these protestations, Nimoy was really not too keen on reprising the role of Spock. A great deal of his reasons was derived from the fact that the shooting of *Star Trek: The Motion Picture* had been a harried and unpleasant experience. The producers, he felt, had not used the characters or concepts well at all, and it was only with extreme reluctance that he now approached a second *Star Trek* movie. Although he will not admit it today, Nimoy may have been the originator of the idea to kill off Spock in the second feature. At any rate, the idea did not give him much pause at all. Perhaps in shedding Spock for good, he figured he might be able to pursue other career goals.

News of this leaked out early and caused great consternation among die-hard *Star Trek* fans. Some of them went so far as to take out an ad in a major Hollywood trade paper predicting that Paramount would lose upward of twenty million dollars, largely from a fan boycott, if it went through with what they considered murder, albeit of a fictional character.

They were dead wrong.

For one thing, Paramount kept tight reins on *Star Trek II*'s budget; it only cost thirteen million to make, less than a third of the maximum estimates of the first film's cost; on the other hand, it grossed eighty million in its initial domestic release alone. Paramount definitely made a big-time profit on *Star Trek II: The Wrath of Khan.*

Hedging its bets over the Spock issue, the studio introduced a new (backup?) Vulcan character, Lieutenant Saavik, portrayed by Kirstie Alley. As director they hired Nicholas Meyer, a successful novelist (*The Seven-Per-Cent Solution*) turned movie director (*Time After Time* and the TV movie *The Day After*), who brought a deft directorial hand and a humanizing touch to the proceedings. (His first film was a childhood effort, an 8-millimeter production of *Around the World in Eighty Days* financed by his father.) Altering the color scheme of the *Enterprise* sets and adding such sensible, human details as "No Smoking" signs and fire extinguishers as well, Meyer was determined not to repeat the mistakes of the first movie. Still, he was a bit surprised to be involved at all:

> "Well, I never was anybody's first choice. . . . I accepted it because I wanted to make *Conjuring* and they said, 'Make a big hit movie and you can do what you want.' Then I saw the first *Star Trek* film—they showed it to me—and I thought I could make a better movie than this."

In spite of this inauspicious beginning, Meyer cared about the TV series, and felt that its uniqueness stemmed from the *Enterprise* crew and the actors who played them. He wanted to treat the characters seriously and use them to explore deep subjects like aging and death. In spite of his regard for the TV actors, however, Meyer had a little trouble getting them to adapt to the scope of the story line.

Unlike the series, where everything returned to normal at the end of an hour, *Star Trek II* would have the characters change and age. Meyer tried other ways to bring more humanity to the bridge: he wanted the crew to smoke and drink coffee. Kirk gets glasses, and is seen reading. Meyer confessed to being thrilled when he learned that Kirk had been based on C. S. Forester's naval hero, Captain Horatio Hornblower, and used the comparison to give depth to his vision of *Star Trek II:* "In fact, I made everyone watch the movie, the one with Gregory Peck and Raoul Walsh."

Special effects this time around were provided by Industrial Light and Magic, the effects company that grew out of George Lucas's *Star Wars* projects. Production began on November 9, 1981 and wrapped on January 2, 1982; after postproduction work was completed, the film was released on June 4, 1982. Says Meyer of his experience: "Making the film was very, very hard. One of the hardest things I ever did." With only five months before release, the film was on a tight schedule, and Meyer lived and breathed the project, working so hard in screening and editing rooms that he didn't see the light of day for six weeks.

Coordinating the visuals and the sound, all going on simultaneously, was an enormous and a tricky task, and Meyer retains a sense of wonder that it all came together, particularly after the battles about the soundtrack: "The process of making this film was that of turning the studio around and convincing them that we were going to do a class act and an event. Slowly, inch by inch, piccolo by violin, cello by trumpet, they retreated and gave ground."

Star Trek II begins when the crew responds to a distress call from the ship *Kobayashi Maru*, trapped in the Neutral Zone. Klingons attack and disable the *Enterprise*, and the crew is ordered to abandon ship. At this moment, the walls slide open and Admiral Kirk steps in: this has been a training simulation of a no-win situation.

Meanwhile, Captain Clark Terrell of the U.S.S. *Reliant* and Commander Chekov are scouting a planet as a possible site for the mysterious Genesis project. Khan Noonian Singh, exiled in the TV episode "Space Seed," appears, and recognizing Chekov uses a brain parasite to learn the two men's mission—and the whereabouts of his nemesis, James T. Kirk. Khan commandeers the *Reliant* and heads for Regula 1, where the Genesis project is being developed by Dr. Carol Marcus and her son David (who doesn't know he is Kirk's son).

Kirk gets wind of something being amiss at Regula 1 and, assuming command of his old ship and crew, sets out to investigate. Senior officers learn that Genesis is a "terraforming" project that can transform a barren world into a flourishing garden, effectively creating life.

When Khan attacks and damages the *Enterprise*, he reveals his identity. Kirk bargains his life—plus the Genesis project—for his crew's safety, but the *Enterprise* is able to damage the *Reliant* and get to Regula 1. Amid the devastation there, Kirk finds Chekov and Terrell, who explain Khan's actions. Kirk and McCoy beam to a nearby asteroid, where they are joined by Dr. Marcus and David, Chekov, and Terrell.

They all appear to be trapped inside this asteroid, with Spock taking the *Enterprise* back to a starbase for repairs. It looks like another no-win situation, like the *Kobayashi Maru* scenario. Asked how he beat the *Maru*, Kirk admits he reprogrammed the simulator, and reveals that Spock's departure with the ship was a ruse. Rescued by the *Enterprise*, Kirk engages Khan in a nearby nebula cloud. Khan is mortally wounded, but launches the Genesis device before he dies.

Kirk orders warp speed, but Scotty is unconscious, with the ship still disabled. Spock decides to enter a highly radioactive area to repair the damage, giving his own life in order to provide warp power. A full funeral is given and Spock's body is launched, in a photon torpedo casing, to the newly born Genesis planet below.

Originally, Spock's death occurred midway through the movie, a placement altered by director Meyer:

"I said he has to die at the end because there is no way you're going to top it. The movie is going to be anticlimactic if he dies in the middle, so I said he should die at the end."

With such an overwhelming climax, interest was immediately focused on the next picture. Was Spock *really* dead—and what part, if any, would Leonard Nimoy have in the next production? He was certainly approached about it by the studio, although this information was kept under wraps until Paramount devised a means of linking Nimoy with *Star Trek III*—without revealing anything about the status of Spock.

During negotiations for *Star Trek III,* Leonard Nimoy rather offhandedly suggested that he thought he could direct as well as either of his predecessors, as he knew the basic material a bit more intimately than they did. To his surprise, producer Harve Bennett thought it was a good idea: and so a directorial career was launched, almost by accident.

Of course, from a marketing standpoint, it was a brilliant move. With Spock dead, *The Search for Spock* could be advertised using Leonard Nimoy's name—while at the same time preserving the mystery of the beloved Vulcan's ultimate fate. Nimoy's return was further brightened by a new enthusiasm for *Star Trek* brought about by a more positive experience on the previous film. The unpleasantness of the first feature was a matter of the past, as the cast had a great time under Nicholas Meyer's direction, and had finally regained the camaraderie that was sadly missing from the first big-screen voyage.

The Search for Spock begins with a replay of Spock's final moments. Kirk and the *Enterprise* are headed back to Earth, where Kirk is faced with the dreary prospect of a deskbound job. Dr. McCoy is behaving strangely, speaking in Spock's voice and questioning Kirk's decision to leave Spock's body on Genesis. Then he collapses.

At space dock, the crew members are to be dispersed to new assignments, but they first gather in Kirk's quarters, reminiscing. Spock's father, Sarek, arrives, accusing Kirk of throwing away his son's life: Sarek believes that Spock entrusted his soul to Kirk just before his death. A quick search of *Enterprise* records shows he had really entrusted it to McCoy.

Meanwhile, the Klingons have learned about the new Genesis planet, and Commander Kruge plans to use its vast power for his own ends. On Genesis, Dr. David Marcus and the Vulcan Lieutenant Saavik discover Spock's empty coffin. They also discover a naked Vulcan child—Spock's body has been revived by the Genesis effect, and is aging in sudden leaps. David and Saavik try to notify the ship, but it is destroyed by Kruge, now entering the system. David admits that because he used unstable materials in Genesis, the planet is about to destroy itself—and them.

Kirk reassembles his crew and steals the *Enterprise,* pursued, briefly, by the *Excelsior.* But Scotty, posted to the *Excelsior*, has disabled the newer ship, and the *Enterprise* is free.

In orbit above Genesis, the *Enterprise* battles Kruge's ship. Kruge reveals his hostages, David and Saavik. Kirk surrenders the *Enterprise*, but initiates the autodestruct sequence, exploding both the ship and the Klingon boarding party. David is killed by the Klingons before seeing his father.

Kirk and crew escape in the Klingon vessel, leaving Kruge on the dying planet. When they arrive at Vulcan,

High Priestess T'Lar rejoins Spock's body and soul. Spock at first does not know his old comrades, but with Kirk's help gradually remembers his life and his friendships, and is on his way to a complete recovery.

Star Trek III's cost and profits were right in the same range as those of the second feature, so there was no doubt that there would be a fourth picture, and Leonard Nimoy was signed to direct once more, becoming the first person to direct more than one film in the series.

An initial script draft was completed in August 1985 by the writing team of Steve Meerson and Peter Krikes. Another factor loomed as well: Paramount Pictures' biggest box-office draw, comedy superstar Eddie Murphy, appeared to be keenly interested in being in the film. Rumors abounded; many feared, and perhaps rightly, that Murphy would dominate the movie at the expense of the regular characters. Still, a role was written with him in mind—though it could have, in a pinch, been played by anyone.

Eventually, Murphy's attention turned elsewhere, and just as well, perhaps, as the combination of these two hot properties—Murphy and *Star Trek*—in one movie would not really have made as much money as two separate projects involving them on their own.

The script was later rewritten by producer Harve Bennett and Nicholas Meyer—the serious parts apparently by Bennett, the humorous ones by Meyer. All four writers received screen credit after the Writers Guild of America determined that all parties had contributed significantly to the project. Director Nimoy had some input as well, particularly in the choice of whales as the focus of the plot.

The rough equivalent of the Eddie Murphy role became that of Dr. Gillian Taylor (Catherine Hicks), the focal twentieth-century character. The movie also promised to feature the largest number of ·*Star Trek* alumni in any of the motion pictures; not only did Dr. Chapel, now a commander (Majel Barrett), and Commander Janice Rand (Grace Lee Whitney) make their first appearances since *Star Trek: The Motion Picture,* but Sarek (Mark Lenard) and Amanda (Jane Wyatt) were on hand to check up on their son's well-being.

The Voyage Home begins with an alien probe, traveling through space and beaming an indecipherable message. It soon renders a number of starships defenseless, and arriving at Earth, directs its signal toward the oceans. Boiling seas and atmospheric disturbances blot out the sun—Earth is helpless.

Our heroes are still at Vulcan, with the stolen Klingon bird-of-prey, renamed H.M.S. *Bounty* by McCoy. Spock completely recovered from his death, the *Enterprise* crew returns to Earth, only to find the planet overwhelmed by the power of the probe. Spock is able to unravel the probe's message, and discovers that it is trying to communicate with humpback whales—extinct for centuries.

Only another whale can communicate with and disable the device—so the *Bounty* uses the classic "whiplash around the sun" timesling technique to travel back in time and capture a whale. The maneuver succeeds, and the cloaked bird-of-prey lands at San Francisco's Golden Gate Park. Spock goes out to communicate with whales, Kirk with attractive marine biologist Dr. Gillian Taylor. Scotty, McCoy, and Uhura, trying to complete the holding tank, have their own adventures in twentieth-century California, and Chekov is captured by Marines and injured.

Dr. Taylor discovers Kirk's secret, and is beamed aboard the ship. Time is running out, but McCoy rescues Chekov, and the *Bounty* chases the whales to Alaska and rescues them from hunters. The timesling is reversed, and the bird-of-prey once more arrives in San Francisco— only now in the twenty-third century. Crashing into the bay, it releases the whales, but the crew barely gets out of the sinking ship alive.

As Spock predicted, the singing whales reassure the alien probe, and the attacks on Earth cease. All charges against the *Enterprise* crew are dropped in light of their heroic efforts to save Earth. Dr. Taylor is welcomed, and with her knowledge of whales is able to join a science vessel.

Starfleet still wants to punish Kirk somehow, and demotes him to captain. His ship—the new Constellation-class *Enterprise*, NCC-1701-A.

But even as Kirk and crew prepared to take charge of their new vessel, yet another *Enterprise* was being launched, with a bald-headed Frenchman as captain, a woman doctor, an android science officer, and, horror of horrors, a *Klingon* on board! Many thought it couldn't, or perhaps even *shouldn't,* happen, but Gene Roddenberry was going to give it one heck of a shot: a *Star Trek* series with an all-new cast, set (somewhat vaguely) seventy-five or so years after the original series, and featuring the *Enterprise* of that farther future, the fifth of its line, NCC-1701-D. Paramount was banking that a syndicated show would generate it revenues, as well. It seemed impossible. But . . . it happened.

CHAPTER EIGHT

A NEW GENERATION EMBARKS

For his new *Star Trek* series, Gene Roddenberry worked hard to produce a show that was true to the ideals of the first *Star Trek,* but had its own unique flavor. As might be imagined, it took some doing; some of the characters took their time settling in, but once they did, they were quite believable.

For starters, there was Captain Jean-Luc Picard. An older, more seasoned officer and a well-trained diplomat, Picard was almost the antithesis of the impetuous hothead James T. Kirk. Picard's low-key style fit well with the twenty-fourth century Federation, which was more interested in peaceful research than hostile confrontations.

Picard has high moral and ethical standards, and a clear vision of Starfleet's purpose in the galaxy. He demands the same from his crew, and as *Star Trek: The Next Generation* develops, the moral dilemmas of the

Enterprise crew often mirror the events of the show's action. The Prime Directive, which prohibits Starfleet from participating in or influencing planetary events, seems to keep starships on a frustratingly tight rein that sometimes taxes even the ethical Picard.

The captain of the *Enterprise* is not lacking in personal courage, however, and is ready to sacrifice self and ship if necessary. As the series grows, we eventually learn of a younger Picard, not unlike the legendary Kirk, who loves danger, likes combat, and takes reckless risks. At the same time, this Frenchman with an English accent reads Shakespeare and detective fiction, loves horses, and has a passion for archaeology. Married to his career, Picard is somehow still a romantic hero, even appearing on the cover of *TV Guide* as the sexiest man on television.

He is a new kind of hero, so different from Kirk, yet completely at home on his *Enterprise*. Many *Star Trek* fans promptly split when he assumed the helm, and fantasized a fight between Kirk and Picard to decide who was the better captain!

For this demanding role, Roddenberry cast British actor Patrick Stewart, who had some movie credits but was best known for his stage performances.

Stewart reveals that he was "compelled" to go into acting "as the result of an argument." Working as a newspaper reporter while rehearsing for amateur plays, Stewart had trouble balancing the two vocations:

"I was always faced with either covering an assignment or attending an important rehearsal or performance. I used to get my colleagues to cover for me, but often I would just make up reports. Finally, I was found out. I had a terrific row with the editor, who said, "Either you decide to be a journalist, in which case you give up all of this acting nonsense, or you get off my paper.' I left his office, packed up my typewriter, and walked out."

He then found work selling furniture!

Enrolling at the famous drama school the Bristol Old Vic, the young Stewart developed skills to match his passion, but was still a little unsure of his abilities:

"When I was younger, I used to think in terms of how I could disguise myself in roles. Now I want my work to say something about me, contain more of my experience of the world."

Success came on the stage, where Stewart was praised for *Who's Afraid of Virginia Woolf?* for which he earned the prestigious London Fringe Best Actor Award. An associate of the Royal Shakespeare Theater Company, Stewart has also played the title roles in *The Merchant of Venice, Henry IV, King John, and Titus Andronicus.*

Stewart was acclaimed for the BBC productions *I, Claudius* and spy novelist John LeCarre's *Smiley's People* and *Tinker, Tailor, Soldier, Spy.* On the big screen, some of Stewart's work includes Gurney Halek in *Dune,* King Leodegrance in *Excalibur,* and Dr. Armstrong in *Lifeforce.*

In spite of his varied and respected background, Patrick Stewart seems to have come by the *Star Trek* role almost by chance. Visiting a British friend in Los Angeles, he appeared on stage at UCLA, where he caught the eye of supervising producer Robert Justman and Gene Roddenberry. Even when not speaking, the actor had such presence he seemed to focus attention on himself. Roddenberry's philosophical hero, Captain Picard, had been found.

With Commander William T. Riker, the role of first officer is expanded. One thing Picard would almost never do is beam down to an uncharted, possibly hostile planet. No twenty-fourth-century vessel or force would risk its commander in such a foolhardy manner; Kirk was, in all frankness, often a reckless fool who, in real life, would have wound up dead as quickly as those red-shirted characters who served as phaser fodder on the old show.

Realizing this, Roddenberry in essence split the command function in two, providing Picard with an executive officer, William Riker, referred to by Picard by the ancient nautical phrase "Number One." (The same term used by Captain April for his first officer in the original pilot "The Menagerie.") Riker, a canny poker player, is not afraid to take risks, but he weighs them carefully, one of his primary responsibilities being the safety of his superior officer.

Some fans insist that Kirk's famous masculine charm was also assigned to Riker, who can always be counted on to find and get to know a beautiful woman. But Riker, like Picard, is highly ethical, and even handles working with his ex-lover, counselor Deanna Troi, with considerable skill. He usually reserves his flirting for non-*Enterprise* crew, and is known on board as a good friend as well as an excellent officer.

Jonathan Frakes, a seasoned television actor was excited about the role: "I knew this was a real part, a big one, and I had to get it." Frakes's sheer determination may well have impressed Roddenberry. Frakes has said, "Gene is so very non-Hollywood and really quite paternal. One of the things he said to me was, 'You have a Machiavellian glint in your eye. Life is a bowl of cherries.' I think Gene feels that way, which is why he writes the way he does. He is very positive, and Commander Riker will reflect that."

If Riker's life is a bowl of cherries, he works hard to make it so: "[Riker is] strong, centered, and somewhat driven. His job is to provide Captain Picard with the most efficiently run ship and the best-prepared crew he can," says Frakes.

Although he considers *Star Trek* to have been a step up, Jonathan Frakes never seemed to have trouble finding work. He appeared on *Falcon Crest, Paper Dolls,* and *Bare Essence,* and was a regular on the daytime drama *The Doctors.* Work on the TV movie of *The Nutcracker* and the critically acclaimed miniseries *Dream West,* plus the miniseries *North and South* gave Frakes more exposure. Roles on and off Broadway rounded out his career.

A native of Philadelphia, Jonathan Frakes briefly attended Penn State before moving on to Harvard. After several seasons at Penn's Loeb Drama Center, he moved to New York:

> "I gave myself a five-year limit. If I wasn't making a living at acting in five years, I would find something else to do. After a year and a half of being the worst waiter in New York and screwing up my back as a furniture mover, I got a role in *Shenandoah* on Broadway and then landed a part in *The Doctors.*"

Moving to Los Angeles in 1979, Frakes began working in TV series:

> "I really have been very lucky. There's a cliché in this business that says, The easy part of being an actor is doing the job; the hardest part is getting the job."

Jonathan Frakes still lives in Los Angeles, and unlike the career officer he plays, has found time to marry: wife Genie Francis plays Laura on the soap opera *General Hospital.*

The *Enterprise* NCC-1701-D has a new bridge position, filled by Counselor Deanna Troi. While ship's counselor can be any Starfleet officer with proper training, Troi's Betazoid heritage gives her considerable empathic powers. Half human, she is sometimes torn by her dual heritage (a recurring *Star Trek* theme). Stunningly beautiful, Counselor Troi is respected for her intelligence, perception, and compassion, which earns her a vital role in Captain Picard's decision-making process. Her "Captain, I sense . . ." quickly became as familiar as "Scotty, take us out of here" or "I'm a doctor, not a . . ."

Deanna's history unfolds throughout the series, and we even meet her mother, the imposing but vivacious Lwaxana Troi, played by Majel Barrett (who is once again the voice of the *Enterprise* computer). Deanna and Riker quickly come to terms with their past relationship, but maintain a special friendship on the show.

Deanna's presence reveals one of the biggest changes from *Star Trek*'s first series. While the *Enterprise* still boldly goes where no one has gone before, her ability to understand and communicate with other beings illustrates the new Federation's peaceful nature. Of course, Deanna's ability to sense the desires of Romulans and Klingons often gives Picard an edge in battle, too!

Like Patrick Stewart, Marina Sirtis hails from Great Britain, but her accent on the show is nothing like his: speaking like no one else seems to reinforce Deanna's half-alien nature. Sirtis appreciates the irony of being British, working in America, and playing an alien. Roddenberry has revisited the idea of a Starfleet officer struggling with a heritage that is both human and alien: part of both worlds, but not quite at home in either.

Troi may have it easier, as times have changed. Sirtis declares:

> "In the twenty-fourth century, geographical or nationalistic barriers are not so evident. The Earth as a planet is your country, your nationality."

Initially auditioning for the role of Security Officer Tasha Yar, Sirtis was suddenly asked to read for Deanna. She recalls that director Corey Allen approached her saying, "You have something personally that the character should have—an empathy. So use it." Sirtis continues, "I love being able to play someone who is so deep with that kind of insight into people, particularly since I usually get cast as the hard 1980s stereotype."

Marina Sirtis was born in North London, to Greek parents. Showing an early interest in performing, she used to sing to passengers on buses. But her parents thought show business wasn't a serious pursuit, so Marina had to act secretly in applying to the Guild Hall School of Music and Drama. After graduating, she landed the role of Ophelia in a repertory company production of *Hamlet.*

Sirtis followed her debut with a few years in British television, musical theater, and repertory work throughout England and Europe. She landed supporting roles in feature films such as *The Wicked Lady* with Faye Dunaway and *Death Wish III* opposite Charles Bronson.

Moving to the U.S. for *Star Trek,* Sirtis settled in Los Angeles. But she still keeps up with her local London soccer team, in which she owns a few shares. Her brother is a professional soccer player.

Marina Sirtis's first experience with outer space was not the *Enterprise*—she is certain she once saw a UFO: "I was working with a repertory company in Worthing, a seaside town in England. One night as I was walking down the street, I saw this huge orange thing in the sky. At first I thought it must be the moon, but it was very off-color. It was very close, but too high to be a balloon. Apparently a lot of other people saw it, too." Too bad Sirtis didn't have Deanna's talent for communicating with aliens!

Most controversial at the show's inception was the android science officer Data, whom many saw as a transparent Spock substitute. While one can find many similarities between the two, there is at least one crucial distinction: where Spock wants to get rid of his emotions and not be human at all, Data's dearest dream is to become *more* human. Whereas Spock has emotions that are subdued but still lie latent beneath his stoical surface, Data, quite literally, has none. Intrigued by humans, Data strives, as a complete outsider, to understand them, and hopes to cultivate emotions of his own.

Several *Next Generation* episodes open with crew members playing poker, providing us with pre-action insight into the characters. While Data may think he is making a scientific study of the game, his poker cronies clearly enjoy his company and consider him as much a friend as any human. Data joins in other crew recreation activities, and even imbibes in food and drink, though he has little sense of taste. Learning from Picard a love of Shakespeare and detective stories, Data becomes more human as the show progresses, and is regarded by his shipmates as a true, reliable friend.

Other human traits that Data has no trouble exhibiting are loneliness, wonder at his origin, and the desire for children, and some of *The Next Generation*'s best episodes explore Data's personal growth.

In the first season, however, Data is still a mystery. He has clearly earned his Starfleet commission, graduating with top honors from the academy, but we learn little else, and share Riker's concern about his fitness for duty. Data will have to prove himself, both to his superiors and to his *Star Trek* audience.

In the words of actor Brent Spiner, who gives the android that strange combination of computer and human life,

"As the series opens we don't know much about Data, only that he was constructed by beings on a planet which no longer exists. He's the only thing left. His creators programmed him with a world of knowledge—he's virtually an encyclopedia—but only in terms of information, not behavior. He's totally innocent. However, he does possess a sense of question and wonder that allows him to evolve. His objective is to be as human as possible."

Brent Spiner believes in extraterrestrials. "Obviously I'm from another planet," he jokes, while admitting that his belief in life beyond Earth is real.

Born in Houston, Texas, Spiner was drawn to the cinema at a young age, watching an average of three movies a day between the ages of eleven and fifteen.

> "At fifteen I was already a major film buff. I could quote lines from movies, tell you who was in it and what year it was made. I always fantasized about being an actor. I was also lucky enough to have a brilliant teacher in high school named Cecil Pickett, who was capable of seeing potential, nurturing it, and making me aware of it."

A walking movie database at fifteen, it's no surprise Brent Spiner seems born to play the endlessly knowledgeable android.

After college, Spiner worked off Broadway, doing "gritty, ugly plays." Says the actor, "The one that finally pushed me over into the serious-actor category was a public theater production of *The Seagull* for Joseph Papp." More roles followed, including the Broadway musicals *Sunday in the Park with George, The Three Musketeers,* and *Big River,* based on Mark Twain's novel *Huckleberry Finn.*

Continuing with his theater roles in Los Angeles, Spiner did *Little Shop of Horrors* at the Westwood

Playhouse. He worked with Woody Allen in the film *Stardust Memories,* and his TV credits include work on the series *The Twilight Zone, Hill Street Blues, Cheers,* and *Night Court.*

On *Star Trek: The Next Generation,* the versatile Brent Spiner plays not only Data, but over time also becomes Data's twin brother Lore, and even his own creator, Dr. Noonien Soong.

An *Enterprise* without a ship's doctor, of course, would have been unthinkable, so Roddenberry provided one in the person of Chief Medical Officer Dr. Beverly Crusher. An intelligent, compassionate, dedicated doctor, she combines her rigorous position with the responsibilities of raising her precocious son, Wesley Crusher.

Beverly's late husband, Jack Crusher, was killed under the command of his longtime friend, Jean-Luc Picard; it was Picard who broke the news to the bereaved family. But after some initial discomfort, Beverly Crusher has no problems working with Picard—and the possibility of a romance between these two major characters intrigues many viewers.

Bones McCoy left Dr. Crusher with some big shoes to fill, but Beverly, like her predecessor, insists on being an active member of the crew. She joins away teams regularly, and can take over command of the *Enterprise* if the need arises. Her keen mind seems to enjoy curing impossible diseases, and if she is sometimes more at home understanding a virus than her own son, this adds depth to her character. A striking woman, Dr. Crusher attracts some strange interstellar admirers, but her career often gets in the way.

Dr. Crusher is the first regular television part for actress Gates McFadden. Like many of her fellow cast members, McFadden has extensive stage credits, including work with a touring Shakespeare company. She says,

"When I was ten, my brother and I attended back-to-back Shakespeare for eight days in a musty, nearly empty theater. There were twelve actors who played all the parts. I couldn't get over it—the same people in costumes every day, but playing new characters. It was like visiting somewhere but never wanting to leave."

Other stage performances include the leads in *To Gillian on her 37th Birthday, How to Say Goodbye, Cloud 9* in New York, and *The Matchmaker* at California's La Jolla Playhouse.

McFadden, born in Cuyahoga Falls, Ohio, trained to be a dancer:

"I had extraordinary teachers: one was primarily a ballerina and the other had been in a circus. I grew up thinking most ballerinas knew how to ride the unicycle, tap-dance, and do handsprings. Consequently, I am an oddball to other dancers."

Earning a bachelor of arts in Theater from Brandeis University in Massachusetts, McFadden kept up her dancing while adding acting and mime to her repertoire, and studied in Paris with Jack LeCoq.

Not content to only be on the stage, McFadden directed the choreography and puppet movement for Jim Henson's feature film *Labyrinth* and assisted Gavin Miller in the staging of fantasy sequences for *Dreamchild.* "Those films were my baptism by fire into the world of special effects and computerized props." It's a world McFadden has come to know intimately in the supersleek sick bay of the new *Enterprise.*

Lieutenant Commander Geordi La Forge commands the operations station on the bridge. A highly intelligent engineer, Geordi's quick mind and sheer determination often save the *Enterprise* and its mission from disaster. His sharp mind does not make him cold or distant, and his easygoing manner and sincere approach make him popular with the entire crew. He considers Data to be his best friend.

Geordi La Forge is named for the late *Star Trek* fan George La Forge, whose passion for the show is credited with his long survival in spite of his cerebral palsy. Like his namesake, Geordi has a physical handicap to overcome, but luckily twenty-fourth-century medicine provides him with a high-tech visor to compensate for his blindness. Geordi can see visual ranges invisible to humans, which is an asset for the engineer: he accepts his disability with calmness, understanding the benefits of the visor as well as the pain of being different.

The portrayal of Geordi La Forge was undertaken by actor LeVar Burton, best known as the young Kunta Kinte on the classic miniseries *Roots,* based on Alex Haley's novel of the same name. His TV movies include *Dummy, One in a Million: The Ron LeFlore Story, Grambling's White Tiger, Guyana Tragedy: The Story of Jim Jones, Battered, Billy: Portrait of a Street Kid,* and the miniseries *Liberty.* Film credits include *Looking for Mr. Goodbar, The Hunter* (with Steve McQueen), and *The Supernaturals* (with Nichelle Nichols).

He maintains a strong interest in children's television, and has hosted PBS's highly acclaimed series *Reading Rainbow* since its debut in 1983.

Before becoming an actor, Burton wanted to become a priest, and even entered a seminary at the early age of thirteen. By the age of fifteen, however, he had discovered the world of philosophy, and gave up his sacramental ambitions. The closest thing to being a priest, he reasoned, was becoming an actor (as DeForest Kelley has said, a good preacher must be a good actor!), a goal he pursued with great vigor. He received superlative reviews for his work in *Roots,* which launched his career.

Says Burton of landing the *Roots* role: "I think the producers had exhausted all the normal means of finding professional talent and were beating the bushes at the drama schools."

LeVar Burton was born in Landsthul, West Germany, son of an army photographer father and a mother who was both an educator and a social worker. Burton seems to have inherited from his parents Geordi's intellectual curiosity and compassionate heart. Still single, Burton lives in Los Angeles with his German shepherd, Mozart.

Tasha Yar, says actress Denise Crosby of her character,

> "comes from an incredibly violent and aggressive Earth colony where life was a constant battle for survival. She can fight and knows her job, but she has no family, is emotionally insecure, and somehow feels that she doesn't quite belong on this ship of seemingly perfect people."

Nevertheless, her crisp manner, fierce loyalty, and dedication to duty make Tasha Yar welcome on the bridge of the *Enterprise*.

Unable to get very close to many of the crew members, Tasha forms a special friendship with Data, and in one very special episode they learn a lot about each other. . . .

Her upbringing as the granddaughter of Hollywood legend Bing Crosby evidently prepared Denise for the unusual life of her character: "Growing up with that wasn't exactly normal or typical either and I think this helps me understand Tasha's imbalance and insecurities."

Before embarking on an acting career, Crosby worked as a runway model in Europe, and fell in love with London. Home on a Christmas holiday, she almost landed her first film role, but says, "My hair was about a quarter of an inch all the way around. I wore army fatigues and no makeup." Casting specialist Toni Howard saw through the grunge, however, and encouraged Crosby to take acting classes.

The effort paid off, and Crosby appeared in *48 Hours, Arizona Heat, The Eliminators, The Man Who Loved Women, Trail of the Pink Panther,* and *Miracle Mile.* On television, she appeared on *L.A. Law, Days of Our Lives, The Flash,* and the TV movies *O'Hara, Stark, Malice in Wonderland,* and *Cocaine: One Man's Poison.* Crosby has been seen on the L.A. stage in *Tamara,* and the controversial one-act play *Stops Along the Way,* directed by Richard Dreyfuss.

While Tasha Yar is killed off in the first-season episode "Skin of Evil," her story is by no means finished, and Denise Crosby and her character are at the center of a major *Star Trek* mystery by the end of *The Next Generation*'s fourth season.

The most shocking member of the new crew is Lieutenant Worf, a Klingon. While there has been peace between the Klingons and the Federation since Kirk's heyday, new audiences are not the only ones who find Worf's presence on the bridge odd. Worf runs into trouble with narrow-minded humans, Romulans, and even Klingons during his journeys.

Worf as a child was the lone survivor of a Romulan attack on the Klingon outpost of Khitomer. Rescued by Starfleet and raised by Russians on Earth, Worf, like other crew members, is a product of two cultures, and while he insists that his first loyalty after Starfleet is to the Klingon Empire, his aggressiveness is tempered by his often hidden personal compassion and his belief in higher ideals. The only bridge officer to have many conflicts with Captain Picard, Worf nevertheless reveres his captain.

Worf's upbringing has made him more like Spock than Data is. He is torn between two cultures, a warrior Klingon dedicated to his own culture but tempered by exposure to human ideals. Worf was added after the pilot for *The Next Generation* and so does not appear in "Encounter at Farpoint." For a while, he would be little more than a grouchy guy with lots of hair standing in the background recommending aggressive action. However, he would soon be featured in more and more episodes, eventually opening up a window on the fascinating world of the Klingon people. (This was no more than a matter of speculation in the days of Kirk.)

As *Star Trek: The Next Generation* unfolds, we learn more of Worf's history, and this orphaned Klingon child turns out to be an important player in the Klingon civil war and the politics of the High Council.

Lieutenant Worf would no doubt be pleased to learn that his native tongue is now taught at the prestigious Massachusetts Institute of Technology, where student Trekkers have developed the language further and presented classes in Klingon. Cast as Worf was the six-foot-five actor Michael Dorn. As a longtime *Star Trek* fan, Dorn says that this role

> "was a dream come true—first because I'm a Trekkie, and second, I'm playing a Klingon, a character so totally different from the nice-guy roles I'd done in the past. Worf is the only Klingon aboard the *Enterprise*. That still makes him an outsider, which is okay by me because Worf knows he's superior to these weak humans. But he never lets the other crew members see that, because he's a soldier first and second."

Dorn considers Roddenberry a genius, and praised him for the courage of his optimistic vision of the future, particularly the possibility of peace between the Federation and the Klingon Empire: "Gene (believed) there is good in everybody—even Klingons!"

Born in Liling, Texas, Dorn was raised in Pasadena,

California, a stone's throw from Hollywood. An early love of music led him to join rock bands, but when his father's friend, an assistant director for *The Mary Tyler Moore Show,* suggested acting, Dorn agreed, and landed some small parts on that show.

Worf may have a distaste for dress-up, ("I am not a merry man!" he insists when Q turns him into a Robin Hood hero in "QPid"), but Dorn spent some time modeling before landing a guest spot on the TV show *W.E.B.* Later, he was cast in *CHiPS.*

He has also appeared in *Hotel, Knots Landing, Falcon Crest, Days of Our Lives,* and *Capitol.* Film credits include *Demon Seed, Rocky,* and *The Jagged Edge.*

Says Dorn, "I want to take it one step at a time and do the best work I can do."

With such a varied cast and diverse characters, it was left to the skill of Gene Roddenberry and staff to bring the *Enterprise* crew together and set them off on their first voyage, to boldly go where no one has gone before.

SEASON ONE

As "Encounter at Farpoint" begins, Captain Picard has just been posted to the new *Enterprise* NCC-1701-D, and is on his way to Farpoint Station to rendezvous with his new first officer. On the journey, Deanna Troi senses a powerful mind scanning the ship, who turns out to be the cynical, omnipotent Q, who informs the crew, "You are notified that our kind has infiltrated the galaxy too far already. You are directed to return to your own solar system immediately."

Picard orders a saucer separation, and with the battle bridge goes to face Q, but eventually surrenders his own person to the alien for judgment. Q puts Picard, Troi, and

Tasha Yar on trial for the crimes of humanity, and they are given a test to prove their value.

The test is how they will react to Riker's discovery, on Farpoint, of an alien life-form, held captive on Farpoint by selfish humans. The ingenuity of the entire *Enterprise* crew, working at Farpoint and on the ship, frees the alien, where it joins its mate in space. Q, disappointed that the humans pass his test, warns that they will meet again.

Sadly, "Encounter at Farpoint" kicked off the new series with something less than a bang. The initial story, by D. C. Fontana, had Gene Roddenberry's "Q" plot slapped onto it; the two plots don't even cross over, much less merge. Instead of a genuine two-hour movie, audiences received a poorly shuffled sandwich of two separate stories . . . with no meat in between.

Like *Star Trek: The Motion Picture,* "Encounter at Farpoint" was slow-moving and all too enamored of its own special effects, which featured a saucer/hull separation as a climactic moment. Special effects for this and other first-season episodes were provided by Industrial Light and Magic, but it soon proved too expensive, and other effects teams were sought out. With a per-episode budget of over a million dollars, *The Next Generation* was a major gamble for Paramount.

"The Naked Now" was a virtual remake of "The Naked Time." It reveals a few things about the characters, but not much, beyond demonstrating just how annoying Wesley could be. "Code of Honor" continued this distressing string of similarities to the old show.

"The Last Outpost" introduced the Ferengi as the new villains, but they don't make much of an impression in their initial foray.

"Where No One Has Gone Before," reflecting the new show's lack of gender bias, used Wesley fairly well and introduced the Traveler, an alien who, after a fashion, becomes one with his own mathematical equations and casts the ship into distant, unexplored regions of space.

"Lonely Among Us" had an alien stowaway on the *Enterprise* making trouble—not for the last time, either.

"Justice" condemned Wesley to death for violating a seemingly trivial taboo on a planet of blond fitness fiends.

"The Battle" provided information on how Picard lost his old ship, the *Stargazer*, in a battle with Ferengi; the old nemesis he defeated then shows up with revenge on his mind.

"Hide and Q" brought back Q, and much too soon. Here, he offers Riker powers that tempt the first officer to play god.

"Haven" introduced Deanna Troi's vexing mother Lwaxana, played by Majel Barrett. A muddled plot involving an arranged marriage and a plague ship echoes memories of "For the World Is Hollow and I Have Touched the Sky."

"The Big Goodbye" introduced Captain Picard's passion for hard-boiled detective fiction, as well as the holodeck concept. While Picard is off playing Dixon Hill, private eye in a simulated 1940s San Francisco, a malfunction causes the characters in the program to develop real personalities . . . and real bullets in their guns.

"Datalore" marks the introduction of Data's twin brother Lore. The *Enterprise* investigates the planet Omicron Theta where Data was originally rescued. Data finds the remains of another android and assembles him, but the new android, named Lore, proves radically different from his compassionate brother. Brent Spiner plays both Data and Lore in this episode.

"Angel One" threatens the crew with a deadly plague, but everything works out in the end.

"11001001" found the all-but-empty *Enterprise* being stolen by aliens while Riker and Picard are distracted by a charming woman, Minuet, in a holodeck fantasy. The imaginary Minuet makes quite an impression on Riker, but there's no chance of anything ever really happening between them.

"Too Short a Season" took an Admiral Jameson back to a planet where he resolved a crisis in his youth. The new crisis was really a ruse set up to lure the now-aged Jameson into the vengeful clutches of an old nemesis, but the admiral had ill-advisedly taken a huge dose of an alien anti-aging drug and arrived at his destination in the full vigor of youth. Complications ensue, as his use of the drug violates his prescription.

In "When the Bough Breaks," sterile aliens kidnap seven children—including Wesley—to renew their race. It doesn't work. "Home Soil" and "Coming of Age" are adequate episodes. Things pick up with "Heart of Glory," the first episode to focus on Worf as more than just a grouchy guy who's handy with a phaser. Renegade Klingons fleeing from the Empire try to involve Worf in their rebellion, provoking a serious conflict of interest for him.

After the action-heavy "Arsenal of Freedom," the show suddenly gets relevant in "Symbiosis," in which the medicine one planet provides to keep another from dying of an ancient plague is revealed to actually be a highly addictive drug. "Skin of Evil" kills off Tasha Yar rather offhandedly, then gives her a nice funeral.

In "We'll Always Have Paris," the husband of an old flame of Picard's accidentally triggers time distortions which only Data can cope with; Picard re-creates, on the holodeck, the date where he stood the woman up years earlier.

"Conspiracy" reveals that the Federation has been infiltrated by evil bugs from a distant planet, but Picard gets to the bottom of it and finally gets to use a phaser on someone in the series.

The first season wound up with "The Neutral Zone," a strangely inconclusive episode involving twentieth-century Terrans who experience future shock after being revived from cryonic suspension. The Romulans reappear, probably since the Ferengi were a washout as heavies, but the show's ending is weak and inconclusive, and the season just sort of fizzles out.

SEASON TWO

The second season of *The Next Generation* showed a marked improvement over its first. A number of changes were evident. First, Jonathan Frakes now sported a beard; some viewers, unimpressed by the first season, now used the sight of a clean-shaven Riker as their cue not to watch an episode, while a hirsute Frakes indicated a better-than-average chance of a good episode.

Claiming that Gates McFadden's character just didn't click with the rest of the cast, Roddenberry summarily dropped Beverly Crusher from the roster with an offhand mention of her going off to head Starfleet Medical. Her replacement was another woman, Doctor Pulaski, ably played by Diana Muldaur, a veteran guest star of the original *Star Trek*. Despite Muldaur's fine acting, however, this character definitely did not click at all.

Perhaps the problem was that the crusty, no-nonsense Pulaski was, in many respects, a female Bones McCoy. The character provided some much-needed friction on the bridge, but for some reason this never really came to bear on the plots much, leaving her a somewhat distant and unengaging character.

Another new character also came on board, although she may have been there all along: Guinan, a mysterious alien woman of great age who functions as bartender and freelance counselor in the *Enterprise*'s open lounge, Ten-Forward, serving synthehol, a marvelous brew whose mildly intoxicating effects can be shaken off at will.

The role of Guinan was created for Whoopi Goldberg, who loved the show as a child and was inspired by its message of racial harmony. Goldberg actually sought out a role on the show; she might even have been on the first season if the *The Next Generation*'s producers hadn't felt that her friend LeVar Burton's reference to her interest in the show wasn't serious.

Guinan's background is shrouded intentionally, with tantalizing bits occasionally thrown out that only serve to deepen the mystery. It is known that Guinan's people were scattered when their home world was destroyed by the Borg; it also comes to light that she has had dealings with Q—who is actually somewhat afraid of her. The real strength of the character lies in her great sympathy for all other living creatures—perhaps the reason for her chosen occupation of bartender. Although not featured on a weekly basis, Guinan is a recurring presence in *The Next Generation.*

Whoopi Goldberg described her character Guinan as "a cross between Yoda and William F. Buckley," but she put a lot of herself into the role as well. Growing up in New York, young Whoopi was inspired by the harmonious message of the original *Star Trek,* and especially by Nichelle Nichols.

When Goldberg learned that her friend LeVar Burton would be on a new *Star Trek* series, she asked him to tell Gene Roddenberry that she wanted to be on the program, too—but the producers of *The Next Generation* thought he was joking. A year later, Goldberg took matters into her own hands and contacted Gene Roddenberry; the two worked together to create the mysterious alien bartender who runs Ten-Forward, a popular gathering place for the crew of the *Enterprise.*

Although Whoopi's first showbiz experience took place at the age of eight, there was a large gap in her career, during which time she raised a child. She worked at a variety of jobs, including one in a funeral parlor whose owner had a curious sense of humor, and "initiated" his employees by hiding in a body bin and playing "zombie," scaring them witless in the process. Whoopi was not amused.

By the time the 1980s rolled around, she was active in theater and comedy, working in Southern California with the San Diego Repertory Theater and putting on a number of one-woman shows. (She also washed dishes at the Big Kitchen restaurant, where the menu still carries a special named after her.) In 1985 she got her big break, in Steven Spielberg's film *The Color Purple,* in a role which earned her an Oscar nomination and the Golden Globe Award. Her role as psychic Oda Mae in *Ghost* netted her the Oscar for Best Supporting Actress in 1991 and she continues to work in films.

She has also won an Emmy for her 1986 guest appearance on *Moonlighting,* and starred in the CBS sitcom *Bagdad Cafe* with Jean Stapleton.

She is concerned with the plight of our nation's homeless, and has, with Robin Williams and Billy Crystal, been a prime force behind the annual *Comic Relief* benefit concerts. In 1989, her various charity projects resulted in her being awarded the Starlight Foundation's Humanitarian of the Year.

Still active on stage, Goldberg has performed in *Moms, The Spook Show,* and *Living on the Edge of Chaos,* as well as returning to the San Diego Repertory Theater, a.k.a. The Rep, to take part in fund-raising performances (along with Patrick Stewart) for that organization.

The second season's opening episode was delayed until November by the Writers Guild strike. The first show was based on a script submitted to the once-planned *Star Trek* revival series. Rewritten for the new cast of characters, "The Child" is conceived upon Deanna Troi by an alien entity that wants to learn about humans by becoming one.

The resultant offspring grows at a rapid rate, but must abandon its physical body when it realizes that it is the source of the deadly radiation affecting the safety of its newfound family. A touching if manipulative story, this one gave Marina Sirtis plenty of emotion to work with.

"Where Silence Has Lease" loses the *Enterprise* in a vast void created by a malevolently curious being; curious about death, it plans to examine all the possible ways humans can die. This process should require no more than two thirds of Picard's crew, but this does not deter the Captain from fighting back with his wits.

In "Elementary, Dear Data," Geordi is annoyed by Data's Holodeck Sherlock Holmes simulation, as the android has captured the logic but not the mystery of the stories. So, Geordi programs in an adversary worthy of— in a crucial slip of the tongue—Data, which makes Moriarty a match for the android. The professor, now "real," begins to learn about the *Enterprise*, and eventually kidnaps Dr. Pulaski in a ploy to be granted life outside the holodeck.

"The Outrageous Okona" veered into idiocy as Data tried to learn about humor from a twentieth-century standup comic created by the holodeck. Joe Piscopo guest-starred. The other plot was also weak, focusing on a Romeo-and-Juliet affair involving a pair of vapid interstellar teens.

"The Schizoid Man" was in fact Data, his personality impinged upon by a brilliant, dying scientist who sees the android as his ticket to immortality. The arrogant scientist cannot carry off the masquerade in silence and is soon revealed; getting him to relinquish his second chance at life is another matter entirely, but when he realizes the harm he's done, he returns control to Data and gives up the ghost, as it were.

"Loud as a Whisper" featured a real deaf-mute actor, Howie Seago, as a similarly affected negotiator who communicates through three telepathic companions; when they are destroyed in a senseless misunderstanding, he abandons his mission of peace until Deanna gives him hope again.

"Unnatural Selection" not only subjects Dr. Pulaski to an aging disease like the one in "The Deadly Years," but it solves the problem using the transporter matrix—the same solution used in a similar episode of the animated *Star Trek* series. The only real suspense comes from the difficulty in finding a transporter trace for Pulaski, as she avoids using the device at all costs. Diana Muldaur does a fine job in the only episode that does her character any justice at all.

In "A Matter of Honor," a Federation-Klingon officer exchange program is introduced. Riker seizes the opportunity to serve on a Klingon ship, but quickly discovers how very different Klingon officers are from their Federation counterparts. Riker eats Klingon food, unwillingly attracts Klingon women, fights with colleagues, and mutinies against his captain—all in a brief tour of duty. His final test comes when his ship, the *Pagh*, is damaged by microbes and the Klingon captain, blaming the *Enterprise*, prepares to attack. Riker's honor requires that he stand by the Klingon code even when it endangers his friends, but he is able to avert a battle, maintain his honor, and preserve good relations with the Klingons.

"The Measure of a Man" is essentially a courtroom drama in which an ambitious science officer, intent on disassembling Data to see how he works, questions the android's rights as a sentient being, provoking Picard to mount an eloquent defense (with a little help from Guinan).

"The Dauphin" is a young woman being transported to her home world, where she can, it's hoped, affect the course of a long-standing feud, to which she represents the key. She becomes friends with Wesley, but their romance is hindered by the young lady's shape-shifting chaperone—and the fact that the girl is in fact also a shape-shifter.

"Contagion" in this case is digital, as the U.S.S. *Yamato* is destroyed by a computer program from an alien probe. The same fate threatens the *Enterprise*, as well as a Romulan ship intent on interfering. Data's apparent death provides the key to solving this problem, and Picard is forced to destroy a fascinating alien teleportation device for security reasons.

"The Royale" traps an away team in a strange casino, which turns out to be an illusion created by aliens for the benefit of an injured astronaut. Long after his death, the illusion continues, and Riker and his team cannot get out until they fulfill the plot requirements of the twentieth-century potboiler novel on which the casino's reality is based.

"The Icarus Factor" pits Riker against his competitive and annoying father. The subplot, in which Worf's friends re-create an important Klingon ritual on the holodeck, is far more interesting.

"Pen Pals" puts Data into contact with an alien child via a primitive radio set. When her planet is revealed to be torn by immense seismic disturbances, Data wants to rescue her, but Picard refuses to let him, invoking the Prime Directive. Nevertheless, the allegedly inhuman android is intent upon helping his unseen friend.

Q is a more serious threat than usual in "Q Who," as he hurls the *Enterprise* far into uncharted space—and introduces the crew to the Borg. Guinan and Q are revealed to have met centuries earlier; it is not a cheerful reunion. This episode probably reveals more about Guinan than any other, but as usual, any answers about her only serve to raise more questions.

"Up the Long Ladder" involves a race of clones who

try to obtain genetic material from the *Enterprise* crew in order to revitalize their race. Basically, after numerous generations they're producing shoddy copies of the original settlers. When they steal cells from Riker and some others, things really heat up. Fortunately, an answer to their problem lies right around the corner in an adjacent subplot involving a cargo hold full of displaced rural colonists, inexplicably Irish in accent, who agree to move to the clones' world, as long as the clones can get used to the idea of reproducing by what can only be termed the old-fashioned way.

"The Emissary" is K'Ehleyr, a half-human Klingon woman, who embarks on a tumultuous romance with Worf while trying to help the *Enterprise* rendezvous with a shipload of Klingons about to revive from cryonic suspension. Arriving too late, Picard is faced with a group of Klingons who still think there's a war on. Worf and K'Ehleyr pull off a masterful ruse: the Klingons could never accept that the Federation won the war, so they trick them into believing that the Empire was triumphant. Worf assumes command of the *Enterprise* for this brief but crucial period (deception is an accepted and honored Klingon method of facing a challenge).

In "Peak Performance," Riker must refurbish and command an abandoned frigate in war games against Picard and the *Enterprise*, an aspect of Federation preparedness against a potential Borg threat. With both ships rigged with simulated weapons systems, they are sitting ducks for a Ferengi captain who cannot believe that there is nothing of value hidden somewhere in this peculiar situation. Riker and crew must somehow work their way out of this predicament; fortunately, they were preparing to cheat in the war games, and have an ace up their collective sleeve.

The season fizzles out with a bargain-basement episode, "Shades of Grey." Riker, infected with a deadly virus, dreams scenes from past episodes. (How convenient.) Pulaski saves him, of course, in her last stand as attending physician on the *Enterprise*.

This is a weak, if not downright pathetic, conclusion to a season which improved immeasurably over the first season. Almost any other episode—"Q Who," "The Emissary," or "A Matter of Honor"—would have seen the season out with a bang rather than a whimper.

Still, the show had more than overcome the founderings of its first season, and had proven that it could stand on its own. The next season would be even better.

CHAPTER NINE:

THE OLD GUARD STUMBLES; THE NEW WAVE TRIUMPHS

hile *Star Trek: The Next Generation* continued to pick up steam and to gain recognition, things did not work out quite so well for the classic *Star Trek* characters. *Star Trek V: The Final Frontier,* directed by William Shatner, was a distinct disappointment to filmgoers—and to Paramount Pictures as well.

Part of the problem was the use the characters were put to. Shatner's attempts at humor and character development revealed an unhappy truth: Leonard Nimoy may have known how to utilize the characters he'd been familiar with for over twenty years—but Shatner hadn't learned half as much.

For example, using Scotty to get an extremely cheap laugh by having him bang his head on a bulkhead, after he'd boasted about the extent of his knowledge of the new *Enterprise*, was a far cry from the true character-based humor of *The Voyage Home.*

And although it is possible for someone to hide his feelings for a close associate for years, having Scotty proclaim his attraction to Uhura after two decades of silence produces nothing more than an awkward moment for audiences and cast alike. Shatner's meddling in the script did nothing to smooth its progress; by adding a newfound half brother for Spock, he effectively cut Spock's screen strength in half, while, not coincidentally, strengthening the focus on Kirk as the main character.

But not all the fault lay with Shatner. Paramount, convinced that humor was the key to the success of a *Star Trek* movie (after all, *The Voyage Home* was funny, and *it* made $110 million), insisted on having comedic moments even if they seemed to come out of nowhere.

A promotional tag asking why theaters were installing seat belts that summer (Shatner actually stated that the studio had really considered this ploy!) was intended by Paramount to suggest the excitement *Star Trek V* had to offer, but the question was neatly answered, and most unflatteringly, by a *Starlog* writer: "To keep the audience from leaving!"

Dixie Whatley, a well-known television movie critic, had this to say: "If *Star Trek: The Final Frontier* is indeed the final big-screen effort, it's a rather dismal way to end it all. This *Star Trek* seems to be a futile reach into the past rather than a dynamic soaring into the future."

Strictly from a box-office standpoint, this feature was a washout. Costing $32 million to make, it grossed only $50 million, less than half the take of *The Voyage Home*.

Shatner landed the role of director by pressuring Paramount to give him a shot at it. He'd already received the green light by the time *Star Trek IV* was to be released; the supporting actors were unhappy to note that Shatner seemed almost to be hoping that Nimoy's second film would take a nosedive.

Not only would this make him the potential savior of

the series, but it would give him a chance to cut costs—by dropping everyone but Captain Kirk and Mr. Spock from the script. This scheme was mercifully erased when *Star Trek IV* broke all *Trek* box-office records.

Quick to allay suspicion, Shatner told *Starlog:*

> "The story centers around Kirk, Spock, and McCoy, but I've carefully choreographed special moments for everybody into this film. Nobody was ignored. What I've attempted to do in *Star Trek V* is to establish relationships between characters that haven't been there before. Scotty and Uhura, for example, are doing something a little bit different this time around. But I've taken great pains to have each character do something he or she hasn't done before."

Unfortunately, those "moments" revealed just how limited Shatner's understanding of those characters was.

Nimoy, meanwhile, was enjoying great success as the director of the smash hit *Three Men and a Baby.* When Shatner's negotiations with Paramount Pictures proved sluggish, Nimoy took another job, directing *The Good Mother* for Touchstone Pictures. (The film, starring Diane Keaton, was not a great success, but received perhaps the best critical notices of Nimoy's efforts to date.) This led to another delay in the start-up of *Star Trek V,* prompting Shatner to threaten to do a Spockless feature; but when Nimoy called his bluff, Shatner was forced to admit that he couldn't do it without him. Production was also stymied by the 1988 strike by the Screen Writers Guild, which endured well into the fall of that year.

Even when Nimoy came on board, as it were, things were not destined to run too smoothly. Nimoy didn't think much of Shatner's story idea, which involved Spock's heretofore-unknown brother popping up out of nowhere and commandeering the *Enterprise*. Nimoy even went so far as to tell Shatner that if they filmed the script (outlined by Shatner and scripted by Harve Bennett and David Loughery) as written, they would be laughed off the screen!

According to Nimoy, Shatner's tension was immense; he'd only directed a few episodes of his TV vehicle *T.J. Hooker* before this, and perhaps feared that he was in over his head. Shatner's apprehension was perhaps best described by Nimoy on a *Tonight Show* appearance promoting the film's June 1989 release:

"I gave him one piece of advice the first couple of days of shooting. I said, 'Stop talking so fast.' It's the sign of a first-time director. You come on a stage the first day on the set and you're excited and you've got the adrenaline going and you're nervous and if you want to spot a first-time director, you look for the guy with the sweaty palms and he's hyperventilating and he's talking too fast. He thought that by talking fast it would speed up the schedule, but you couldn't understand a word he was saying."

Of the film's budget, much can be said about its size. Six million apiece to Shatner and Nimoy (for acting only) trimmed the $32 million budget down to $20 million. After the director's salary and the rest of the cast's remunerations, things were pretty slim, and Paramount decided to eschew the use of George Lucas's Industrial Light and Magic's services. Ultimately, the effects for the film's climax were not as effective as they could or should have been.

The final word, ultimately, was in the box-office receipts.

(When *Star Trek V* was released on home video, it was ticketed at $89.95, as opposed to the more reasonable $29.95 price of the previous four features—a blatant effort to get home-video buyers to help make up for the deficit on Shatner's directorial debut.)

Undeterred by early criticism, Shatner has pursued both directing and producing. He recently produced the TV series *TekWar,* based on novels he has written himself.

Close on the heels of this release came the third season of *Star Trek: The Next Generation.* Getting off to an adequate start, this would prove to be *The Next Generation*'s best season yet. Repenting of his dismissal of Gates McFadden—the character of Dr. Pulaski never caught on, and fans wrote in requesting McFadden's return— Roddenberry brought back Beverly Crusher as the *Enterprise*'s chief medical officer. Little mention was made of her tenure as head of Starfleet Medical, and Pulaski was not even referred to; her whereabouts were left unknown. (A treatment devised by Pulaski was referred to in a later episode, however.)

Early in the season, executive producer Rick Berman hired writer Michael Piller, who soon achieved the rank of executive producer himself. His task was to oversee scripts for the show.

Piller was largely responsible for the great improvement in script quality; in fact, he seemed to specialize in finding ways to create engaging stories in spite of Gene Roddenberry's rather stringent format guidelines, which forbade, among other things, even the slightest hint of conflict among members of the *Enterprise* crew. Piller's arrival was a crucial factor in the show's ever-growing vitality.

Also on hand was a new model of the *Enterprise,* a four-foot model which generally supplanted the six- and two-foot models built at the series' inception. This was the work of Dan Curry and Robert Legato, the show's special-effects wizards. Supplanting Industrial Light and Magic early in the first season, they developed new and more flexible ways to present the *Enterprise* using digital visual compositing rather than optical film effects; this approach makes it possible to add a theoretically limitless number of elements to a shot without any loss of image clarity.

As the series proceeded, they built a library of shots that could be altered and reused without any risk of redundancy. As for the new model, it was easier to use than the six-footer, which was, however, the only model with hull separation capacity. The six-footer was also a very complex piece of lighting wiring; the new model simplified things considerably with a flexible neon system. (The windows and interior lights are actually visual effects composited on later in the shooting process.)

SEASON THREE

With these changes in place, the third season revved up with "Evolution," involving one of Wesley's science projects gone awry, as microscopic nanites begin to eat the computer core of the *Enterprise*. A scientist preparing to observe a rare stellar event is perturbed by this interference and tries to kill the by-now sentient creatures, provoking their displeasure. But with Data as an interface, communications are established and things are ironed out.

In "The Ensigns of Command," Data is assigned to get a human colony off a planet before the aliens with legal rights to that world arrive and destroy them. Unfortunately, the humans are determined to stand and fight, and the android officer must use less than tactful means to convince them of just how overwhelming an enemy they are faced with.

Picard, meanwhile, tries to stall the aliens by finding a loophole in their agreement with the Federation, which unfortunately happens to be one of the longest, most exacting documents in history. Meanwhile, Data makes a more-than-scientific impression on a young woman cyberneticist, and learns something about kissing.

"The Survivors," a human man and his wife, occupy a small patch of green on a planet otherwise utterly destroyed by an alien attack. They have no desire to be rescued. An alien ship drives the *Enterprise* off but something in its behavior triggers Picard's suspicions, and he returns.

The ship seems to be trying to keep the *Enterprise* away from the survivors. It turns out that the man is a powerful alien who, posing as human, fell in love on Earth years before and maintained human form when he married. When his wife died in the attack he was so grief-stricken that he used his powers to destroy the aliens—not just the attacking force but the entire race! Guilt-ridden over this genocide, he has exiled himself to this world, creating an illusionary image of his wife, as well as the ship to protect his privacy. Picard wisely leaves him alone to endure his self-imposed exile from the rest of the universe.

"Who Watches the Watchers" casts Picard as an unwilling god when a Federation observation post on a developing world is discovered by the inhabitants. A native, injured in an accident, is beamed up to the *Enterprise* for medical treatment but wakes up long enough to see the captain.

When he returns to his world he brings word of this new god. This causes complications for Riker and Deanna as they search, disguised as the Vulcan-like locals, for a missing member of the observation team. Picard finally beams down to explain that he's only human, but his would-be disciple refuses to take even this at face value. An intriguing episode.

"The Bonding" is another key Worf episode. When a member of an away team commanded by the surly Klingon is killed, the guilt-ridden Worf feels responsibility for the woman's orphaned son. So does an alien entity on the planet, which tries to assuage the boy's loss by re-creating his dead mother. Fortunately, the being is convinced that this would not be in the boy's long-term interests, and the story ends as Worf and the boy undergo a Klingon brotherhood ritual. A good episode despite the alien's motivational similarity to that of the alien in "The Survivors."

In "Booby Trap," Geordi re-creates the woman who designed the *Enterprise*'s warp drive on the holodeck in order to work up a solution to the fact that the ship is trapped by an ancient energy-draining device. This idea works out—but Geordi falls for the illusion of Dr. Leah Brahms.

"The Enemy" finds Geordi stranded on a hostile planet where he must overcome a wounded Romulan's suspicions and gain his trust in order for them both to survive. Another Romulan is taken aboard the *Enterprise*, where a blood transfusion is needed to save his life, but the only compatible donor, Worf, refuses to help, as his parents were killed by Romulans.

"The Price" details negotiations for a potentially valuable wormhole; the Ferengi, now played as completely greed-addled buffoons, crash the negotiations and effectively knock the Federation's negotiator out of the picture by provoking an allergic reaction.

Riker's poker-playing skills lead Picard to make him the replacement negotiator, but the real danger at the table is a secret Betazoid misusing his powers to gain an edge, as well as to romance Deanna Troi. However, he misjudges her, and closes the deal before the wormhole is determined to be unstable.

"The Vengeance Factor" involves Picard in establishing diplomatic relations between a planet and a piratelike band that split away a generation earlier. While transporting the planet's leader, Riker becomes involved with her assistant, who is carrying a genetically engineered poison in her system that is fatal to members of a specific clan. He realizes this in time to save the negotiations, but is forced to kill her to prevent another murder, and is left shaken.

"The Defector" is a Romulan admiral determined to prevent a sneak attack by his empire. Naturally, Picard doubts his story, and it turns out to be a Romulan ploy to capture a Federation ship. But the admiral was sincere, having been used by his own government.

Picard escapes the Neutral Zone trap by revealing a pair of wild cards up his sleeve: he's been accompanied by two cloaked Klingon ships all along. The admiral commits suicide, leaving a heartfelt letter that can never be delivered to his family until the two sides achieve a lasting peace.

"The Hunted" examines the nature of soldiers in peacetime. A planet transformed some of its citizens into perfect soldiers and shipped them off to a sequestered colony once the war was won; the soldiers want their normal lives restored. The *Enterprise* stumbles into the midst of this when the crew helps capture an escaped "prisoner" who is one of these soldiers. In a fitting conclusion, the soldiers and the government are caught in a standoff. Picard invokes the Prime Directive and clears out, leaving this society to work out its problems on its own.

"The High Ground" involves Picard and Beverly Crusher in a terrorist/hostage situation; the terrorists have legitimate grievances but go too far, as does the oppressive government in combating resistance. An intriguing story that loses force by trying to straddle both sides of a difficult and emotionally charged issue, "The High Ground" is essentially the situation in Northern Ireland watered down to the point of inanity and cast in science fiction form.

Q shows up, stripped of his powers by his peers, in

"Déjà Q." Picard takes some convincing that Q is not responsible for his current crisis, which involves a moon with a decaying orbit.

Q learns humility of sorts when an old nemesis of his shows up and threatens the *Enterprise*; he leads it away in a shuttlecraft, and is rewarded for this selfless act with the restoration of his powers.

Needless to say, his humility dries up pretty quickly, but he does save the planet threatened by its moon, forces Picard to listen to mariachi music, and enables Data to enjoy a good laugh.

"A Matter of Perspective" is basically *Rashomon* in space, as the holodeck is used to re-create the varying accounts of a situation in which Riker may have committed murder. Of course, he is cleared of all charges.

"Yesterday's *Enterprise*" introduces a temporal distortion which casts the *Enterprise* into an alternative history where the Federation is losing a long-running war with the Klingons. Since this prevented the crew from meeting the creature in "Skin of Evil," Tasha Yar is back on board, in place of Worf, who's missing for obvious reasons.

Guinan alone senses that something is wrong, and struggles to convince Picard that reality can be changed. The earlier *Enterprise* which has caused the time shift must ultimately go back through the time rift and face its fate. It will be destroyed defending a Klingon outpost from a surprise Romulan attack, thus making peace between the Klingons and the Federation. Tasha, sensing that her death in the other timeline was meaningless, joins the other ship, and normality is restored, with no one but Guinan the wiser.

"The Offspring" is Lal, an android "daughter" created by Data. This is a very touching episode. Suspense is introduced by having the Federation attempt to take her away for study, as in "The Measure of a Man," as if the legal precedent set there had no weight.

Picard is willing to risk his career to protect the androids' rights, but the issue becomes moot when Lal malfunctions and dies, after having developed the emotions her "father" lacks. This marks the directorial debut of Jonathan Frakes, who handles the sensitive emotions of this tale with great aplomb.

In "Sins of the Father," the *Enterprise* crew is in for a rough ride when a Klingon exchange officer, temporarily replacing Riker, is harsh on everyone except Worf. As gentle treatment is a serious insult to a Klingon, Worf is about to challenge the newcomer to combat when he learns the stranger is actually his younger brother, Kurn.

Using the *Enterprise* computer and records from the Federation ship *Intrepid*, a Khitomer witness, Data discovers something is odd about Klingon reports of the massacre. Picard and Riker accompany Worf to the Klingon home world, where they rescue another Khitomer survivor, Worf's nurse. They learn that the real traitor of Khitomer was not Worf's father, but a member of another powerful house.

The Klingon High Council is thrown into an uproar with this news, but cannot clear Worf's family name, lest civil war erupt. Worf and his brother must die. But Worf, raised by humans, chooses the other option—official discommendation and dishonor for himself and his brother. While he sacrifices his personal honor, Worf behaves as a true Klingon, preserving the stability and glory of the empire. He may, one day, clear his family name and again be known as Worf, Son of Mogh.

In "Allegiance," Picard is replaced by a double and himself imprisoned with three other aliens (one of whom is actually one of their captors in disguise). While Picard must try to generate cooperation between his new companions, the *Enterprise* crew must contend with the peculiarities of the impostor. Fortunately, Riker takes command just in time to avert a major disaster.

"Captain's Holiday" leads Picard into trouble and romance, thanks to Riker's mischievous suggestion intended to make the vacation a bit more interesting. Time travelers, Ferengi, and the beautiful if unethical archaeologist Vash provide the staid captain with a week he won't forget, although he doesn't get much reading done, as per his original plan.

"Tin Man" is the name given an alien artifact, apparently a sentient spacecraft. Tam, a Betazoid born with full powers, is assigned to make contact. His telepathy makes it hard for him to avoid the constant mental chatter of most beings, but he becomes friends of sorts with Data, whose mind is closed to him.

When a Romulan craft approaches 'Tin Man," Tam alerts it, revealing the full extent of his mental reach, and it lashes out, destroying the intruder. Ultimately, Tam joins with the spaceship, which was awaiting death by supernova after the death of its crew, and they disappear into the universe, though not before sweeping the *Enterprise* and a second Romulan ship away from the range of the exploding star.

"Hollow Pursuits" introduces the potentially sticky subject of holodeck abuse, as Barclay, a man on Geordi's engineering team, uses the deck to vent his frustrations and explore his fantasies, using his superior officers as characters in his creations. Unfortunately, Barclay's work is suffering, even though he may be very capable of helping solve the *Enterprise*'s latest problem—which he does, once his own problem is discovered and addressed.

A good performance by Dwight Schultz enlivens this intriguing episode; apparently, Barclay is too much the innocent to have used the holodeck in any *seriously* twisted way, even though he obviously has a thing for Deanna.

In "The Most Toys," Data is kidnapped (and his destruction faked) by an avaricious collector. Although intrigued at being filed alongside a Roger Maris baseball card (complete with re-created bubble gum odor,), Data will not comply with his captor's wishes—until a woman is threatened.

The woman tries to help Data escape and dies for her troubles. Data is finally located and beamed away just as he is about to shoot the villain with a disrupter, having concluded that the man will only inflict more pain and death if he is not destroyed. This is an intriguing lesson for the android, who supposedly could not kill in earlier episodes but here admits to being able to use lethal force. Obviously, difficult moral decisions are also within his powers.

Spock's father "Sarek" appears in this episode that bears his name, wherein his vital diplomatic mission is threatened by an encroaching form of senility, rare among Vulcans but overwhelming when it strikes. It induces the Vulcan's strong emotions, long suppressed, to break out, causing turmoil among the crew.

Sarek finds it hard to face the truth, but when he does, a Vulcan mind meld with Picard enables him to finish his task in top form, while Picard valiantly copes with Sarek's set-aside emotions—which include anguish over his relationship with his famous son. This episode also reveals that a young Lieutenant Jean-Luc Picard was actually in attendance at Spock's wedding years earlier.

In "Ménàge à Troi" the Ferengi DaiMon Tog appears to take a liking to Lwaxana Troi, and kidnaps her, Deanna, and Riker. Tog's attempts to seduce Lwaxana quickly give way to his real intent, which is to use her empathic powers to his business advantage. As Deanna looks on, Riker outwits his Ferengi guards, and Lwaxana maneuvers Tog into releasing his prisoners.

"Transfigurations" concerns a wounded, amnesiac alien with strange powers of recovery who strikes an easy rapport with Beverly Crusher. He is pursued by representatives of his culture; remembering himself, he is revealed as a person in the final stages of his race's evolution to a higher form, a metamorphosis ruthlessly suppressed by his government, but he succeeds in moving on, pointing the way for others . . . perhaps, someday, even humans.

After the dismal conclusion to season two, *The Next Generation*'s producers wisely chose to end the third season with a bang-up finale. "The Best of Both Worlds" brings back the Borg, intent on absorbing the Federation and all other life-forms into their machine-hive mind.

The *Enterprise* answers a colony's distress call, only to discover that the Borg got there first. The Federation Borg specialist, the ambitious Commander Shelby, joins the crew to try to defeat the Borg. She is also extremely interested in Riker's job, having learned he has been offered his own command.

In an engagement with the Borg, Picard is kidnapped and transformed into Locutus, a mouthpiece for the Borg Collective. In several horrifying scenes, Picard is transfigured by machines, his mind taken over by the aliens. He threatens the *Enterprise* and all humanity. When Locutus/Picard demands the surrender of the *Enterprise*, Riker must order Worf to fire on the enemy ship.

This cliff-hanger ending left audiences clamoring for more, which was a shrewd move after the two lackluster season finales that preceded it. It was a long summer after "The Best of Both Worlds" brought the season to its end; there was little else for captivated viewers to do but to watch reruns of *The Next Generation* until fall. Where Kirk and crew had slipped on a banana peel the previous summer, Riker, Data, Worf, and their cohorts seemed bound to fly even higher than ever—with or without Picard. (Supposedly, Patrick Stewart was considering leaving the show—the cliff-hanger gave him time to reconsider, it seems.) To top off everything, the fourth season would take the episode count of *The Next Generation* beyond the seventy-nine-show record of its illustrious predecessor, boldly sending it where no *Star Trek* had gone before.

CHAPTER TEN:

THE TORCH IS CARRIED ON

The Next Generation's 1990 season got off to a rousing start with the conclusion to the cliff-hanger ending of season three. The special effects wizards had to dust off the six-foot *Enterprise* for a saucer separation sequence, but this was the least of their triumphs in the opening episode.

SEASON FOUR

As "The Best of Both Worlds, Part II" opens, the attack on the Borg ship fails, causing extensive damage to the *Enterprise*, and the Borg, with Picard's body and mind, resume their course toward Earth.

Warned by the *Enterprise*, the Federation waits with an armada of forty ships, plus Klingons and the possibility of Romulan aid against this unstoppable enemy.

Admiral Hansen communicates via subspace, commissioning Riker as captain. In another message, Hansen is relaying that the Borg have attacked, when he is suddenly cut off.

Struggling to get moving at any speed, the *Enterprise* reaches Earth's solar system in time to witness the horrifying devastation of the fleet. Riker separates the saucer section, and by acting unpredictably confuses the Borg. Picard is finally rescued, and Data creates a neural link to infiltrate the Borg command system. Unbelievably, some shred of the real Picard remains, and in a breathless ending he is able to help his crew destroy the Borg.

"Family" is a direct follow-up to the preceding episode, as a weary Jean-Luc Picard takes some time off at his family estate in France and works out some long-standing grudges with his older brother, a gruff farmer. Wesley finally meets his father via a recorded holodeck message, and Worf is embarrassed when his human foster parents come on board the *Enterprise*. An intriguing character study, this episode works admirably without any life-threatening crises whatsoever.

"Brothers" opens with Data suddenly shifting into a mysterious mode and taking over the *Enterprise*, diverting it to a mysterious planet, and beaming down, leaving a bewildered crew striving to figure out the complex code he entered into the computer—using Picard's voice!

On the planet's surface, Data encounters an aged human who turns out to be Dr. Noonien Soong, Data's creator. Soong has long been presumed dead but actually fled the events described in the first season's "Datalore" and escaped to this distant hideout.

Now he is dying, and has summoned Data to give him a new, improved chip that will provide him with basic emotions; his first attempt, with "evil twin" Lore, didn't work out. Lore himself shows up, since the homing signal also triggered him. Lore is jealous of the attention Data is getting, and tricks Soong into giving him the chip, which causes him to become even more twisted.

Soong dies after being manhandled by Lore, leaving Data no better off than before, and the *Enterprise* is restored to Picard. Some but not all of the discrepancies between the information in this episode and that in "Datalore" can be attributed to the fact that Lore is a liar.

Originally, this story merely had Data meeting his creator, until Michael Piller realized that that provided a rather static scenario, and brought back Lore to spice up the proceedings. Veteran actor Keye Luke, since deceased, was considered for the role of Soong, but it was decided to give Brent Spiner all three roles: a more expensive approach, to be sure, but one that made this a tour de force for the Texan actor.

"Suddenly Human" draws Picard into controversy when he discovers that a teenager found on a damaged alien craft is actually human. Picard tries to reacclimate the boy to human society, but it's a losing battle, with humorous overtones deriving from the Captain's faltering attempts to be a surrogate father.

The boy's Talarian foster father tries to reclaim him, but old injuries revealed by a medical scan lead Picard and crew to assume the possibility of abuse, a touchy issue skirted around here and basically used to provide a stalling device, rather than to have the youth simply handed over to the culture where he belongs. Anyway, it all works out in the end, as the boy decides to continue his life as a Talarian.

"Remember Me" traps Dr. Crusher on an *Enterprise* where the crew is disappearing, but only she notices. Eventually, she and Picard are alone on the bridge, and the captain is reduced to patiently explaining to her that the two of them are all the crew that the ship requires. Actually, she has been trapped in a warp bubble produced in an experiment by her son, who is desperately trying to save her. As the bubble collapses, Crusher, now alone, finds that the universe around her is shrinking, shearing away sections of the false reality she inhabits.

Suspecting the truth, she struggles to get to the engineering section of the construct before it is lost. Wesley's efforts are aided by the arrival of the Traveler from the first season's "Where No One Has Gone Before," who joins Wesley in saving his mother; Wesley actually "phases out" at the controls, as the Traveler once did, and all is set right.

"Legacy" takes the *Enterprise* to Tasha Yar's home world to rescue some captured Federation officers. They are drawn into that planet's long-standing factional war, which has achieved a balance of power that both sides desire to break. One side has a trump card designed to win the help of the *Enterprise* crew, especially Data: Tasha Yar's sister Ishara, who uses the trusting android and almost succeeds in her plan.

"Reunion" brings back Worf's flame K'Ehleyr and continues the Klingon saga. K'Ehleyr acts as an emissary for the dying leader of the Klingon High Council, who wants Picard to find out who has been having him poisoned, and then oversee the choosing of the Council's next leader. After a bomb kills two Klingons during a preliminary ritual, the *Enterprise* crew discovers that the enemy is Duras, who nurses a long hatred of Picard.

The episode's other plot involves Worf's personal life: K'Ehleyr has another surprise—Worf's son Alexander. She agrees to marry Worf in the ancient Klingon ritual, and together they discover that it was Duras's father who betrayed Khitomer. Trying to help Worf regain his honor, K'Ehleyr is killed. In blind passion, Worf murders Duras, but is forgiven when he reveals that K'Ehleyr was his mate. Even with Duras dead, however, Worf's honor cannot be reinstated, lest a civil war erupt in the Klingon Empire. Once again putting the good of his people over his own desires, Worf agrees to keep his secret until he and his brother can set matters right.

"Future Imperfect" finds Riker awakening after sixteen years to find himself the captain of the *Enterprise*, with a son. He has forgotten the sixteen years in question; his last memory is of a visit to a planet, where he was infected by a virus that had lain dormant for years before wiping out all memories accrued since its inception.

On the verge of an important diplomatic mission, he is hard pressed to deal with this reality. The computer is slow to provide records of his missing years, especially those concerning his late wife; when at last he is shown home videos of her, she turns out to be Minuet, the holodeck creation from the first season's "11001001."

This reveals everything to be a sham, and he faces down a bearded Admiral Picard. The bridge fades away, and is revealed to be a Romulan holodeck simulation set up in order to extract information from Riker. His "son" is revealed to be a captured Earth boy. Another adventure ensues, but it too begins to show gaps in its consistency, and Riker realizes that he's being duped again.

The boy is revealed to be an alien child, hidden from enemies by his late parents; the devices they provided him for his protection have also enabled him to create illusions that will enable him to trick Riker into being his friend. But Riker, faced with the truth, takes the child with him, ending his lonely exile. It seems Riker was the right choice for a friend after all.

"Final Mission" is Wil Wheaton's farewell as Wesley Crusher; he and Picard are stranded on a desert world, Picard is wounded, and Wesley must take charge to save the captain's life. The following episode, "The Loss," deprives Deanna Troi of her empathic powers. Although it's a foregone conclusion that she'll get them back within the hour, she does go through some interesting emotional situations in an interesting script.

"Data's Day" is a busy one: in order to help Commander Maddox better understand him, Data sends him a communication describing a "typical" day in the life of an android.

Today, Data is supposed to be best man at the wedding of Chief O'Brien and botanist Keiko, but when Keiko calls off the wedding, Data must learn how to interpret mysterious human emotions in order to reunite the pair.

At the same time, Vulcan Ambassador T'Pel beams aboard. She must travel with utmost secrecy into the Neutral Zone. In the guise of testing Data's security precautions, T'Pel tries to use Data to gain access to secret information. When the *Enterprise* delivers T'Pel to the Neutral Zone, the crew learns that the ambassador had really been a Romulan spy, deep into Federation politics.

Unfortunately, we never learn what Commander Maddox thinks when he hears about Data's "typical" day.

The following episode, "The Wounded," was another intriguing story, with a respected Starfleet officer behaving in strange ways. Captain Ben Maxwell hasn't given up his hatred of the Cardassians, and is trying to restart the war. When a Cardassian ship fires on the *Enterprise*, her crew must locate Maxwell's ship, the *Phoenix*, and prevent her from starting a war. At the same time, Picard must persuade the Cardassians to let Starfleet handle the matter, and uses all his diplomatic skills to convince them.

When the *Phoenix* destroys one Cardassian ship and threatens another, Chief O'Brien draws on his own experience serving under Maxwell in order to get the unhinged captain to back down. Maxwell surrenders. The Cardassians leave, with Picard's warning that the Federation will be watching them.

"Devil's Due" is owed by the people of the planet Ventax II to an entity named Ardra, who provided their once crisis-wracked world with peace and prosperity a thousand years ago; now that the term is up, Ardra appears, replete with earthquakes and shape-shifting powers.

Picard must prove that she's a fraud who's using an ancient social myth for her own ends by taking it literally and scaring the wits out of the Ventaxians. Fortunately, her cloaked ship, with its tractor beams (for the earthquakes) and transporter (for the shape-changing), is discovered and boarded, enabling Picard to briefly assume the interplanetary conwoman's apparent powers long enough to turn the tables and thwart her greedy plan.

"Clues" leaves the *Enterprise* crew with a mystery: how did they lose twenty-four hours? Data knows, but he's not telling. In fact, it takes some time for them to realize the loss, and the fact that Data is concealing the truth from them. When asked why he's doing this, the android reveals the startling truth that he is acting under orders from Picard . . . orders that the captain does not remember giving.

Ultimately, it turns out that Picard had agreed to this peculiar arrangement to protect the privacy of a reclusive alien race. He even agrees to it a second time, but cautions the aliens to destroy all traces of their passing; the first time, there were too many clues left behind, leading the crew to suspect something was amiss. The second cover-up is successful.

"First Contact" breaks with series format in providing a startling look at the questions raised by the *Enterprise*'s techniques of determining a planet's worthiness to join the Federation. Here, we see the *Enterprise* crew as aliens, from the Malcorians' point of view.

Riker has been disguised as a Malcorian, but when he is injured the disguise begins to crumble. With his communicator lost, Riker cannot be easily rescued by the *Enterprise*, and Picard risks beaming down to the planet and contacting the science minister, Mirasta. Mirasta is open-minded, but explains her people are too ethnocentric to accept the Federation. She is correct, and negotiations with other ministers only alarm them, and endanger Riker's situation: one chancellor attempts suicide, trying to place blame on Riker in order to cut off all contact with aliens. Riker's phaser is on stun, however, and its discharge pattern gives the *Enterprise* the opportunity to rescue the first officer.

Both Malcoria III and the *Enterprise* determine the planet is not ready to join the Federation. While the starship's visit will be kept secret on her planet, Minister Mirasta still dreams of space travel, and is granted asylum on board the *Enterprise*.

"Galaxy's Child" primarily involves a space-bred infant that imprints on the *Enterprise* after its mother is inadvertently killed; it attaches itself to the ship and begins to drain power at an enormous rate. Meanwhile, Leah Brahms, whom Geordi "met" on the holodeck in the previous season's "Booby Trap," visits the ship to see her engine designs in operation. She is perplexed but intrigued by Geordi's modifications, as well as by his manner, while Geordi is baffled by the fact that she is nothing like the simulation he worked with. Not only that . . . she's married. When she discovers the holodeck program with her image in it, she goes into a rage. Fortunately, she and Geordi become friends in time to work together and resolve the episode's other plot concern.

"Night Terrors" has the ship's crew going nuts due to sleep deprivation caused by an alien vessel's attempts to communicate telepathically; once Deanna figures out what's going on, it's a piece of cake for the *Enterprise* and the aliens to escape from the space anomaly holding them both captive.

"Identity Crisis" takes Geordi back to a planet he visited as part of an away team from the U.S.S. *Victory* five years before; members of that away team have been vanishing and seem to be headed back to that particular world. Geordi and Susanna, the only other away team member remaining, review the mission records to find out clues, but to little avail.

Susanna and Geordi transform into alien beings but are taken to sick bay; when Geordi changes, he escapes and heads down to the planet. A search ensues, while Crusher tries to isolate the cause of the metamorphosis. Unfortunately, any suspense is undercut by the certainty that Geordi will be saved by episode's end.

"The Nth Degree" features the return of Reginald Barclay who, having recovered from holodeck addiction, is made a superintellect by an alien probe. His mind expands into the ship's computer and takes charge, bringing the *Enterprise* to the center of the galaxy. He is restored to normalcy by a galactic being who explores the universe through having other beings visit him. The payoff is weak, but Dwight Schultz is fun as Barclay, gaining immeasurable confidence, becoming a great actor, making a play for Deanna Troi, and arguing successfully with a holodeck Albert Einstein.

"QPid" features the return of Vash, Captain Picard's romantic interest from "Captain's Holiday." The captain is a bit abashed to find her part of an archaeological symposium on the *Enterprise*, and she is annoyed to find that he's kept mum about their affair to his fellow officers.

Into this volatile situation pops Q, who feels that he owes Picard a favor from their last encounter. Q thus whisks Picard and crew off to a simulated re-creation of the Robin Hood story (it was, after all, the summer of *Prince of Thieves*), where Vash becomes Maid Marian, due to be executed for treason by the Sheriff of Nottingham.

Picard, a reluctant Robin Hood, must rescue her; neither the Captain nor Q have taken into account Vash's keen survival instincts, and discover that she's playing along with the sheriff's marriage plans! Q, fascinated, refuses to interfere before the situation has run its course.

Fortunately, after Picard is captured, the rest of "the Merry Men" stage a rousing escape and Picard gets to duel the villain to the death. Q restores things to normal, and announces that he's found a kindred spirit in Vash; the two don safari garb and blink away to explore the universe, courtesy of Q's cosmic powers. An extremely silly episode, but the cast obviously had fun, and it shows through.

"The Drumhead," Jonathan Frakes's third directorial outing, not only makes more references to *The Next Generation*'s back history, but also presents some criticism of Picard's command.

When a dilithium chamber explodes, and a Klingon exchange officer is accused of sabotage, young medical crewman Simon Tarses is suspected as well. Starfleet Admiral Satie comes to investigate. Her Betazoid aide determines that Tarses is hiding something, and he eventually confesses to Romulan blood. Picard, with a keen sense of justice, tries to prevent what he feels will be a witch-hunt. As a result, both Tarses and Picard are essentially on trial, Picard for violating the Prime Directive. Asks Satie, "Are you sure you have recovered completely from your experiences with the Borg?"

Geordi determines that the explosion was an accident, not sabotage, but it is up to Picard's eloquent reasoning—and clever unveiling of Satie's paranoia—to resolve the crisis and end the trial

"Half a Life" gives Majel Barrett a chance to play Lwaxana Troi as something other than a sex-crazed buffoon, and the result is a very touching episode. Still chasing men, of course, she falls for the alien scientist Timicin (David Ogden Stiers of *M*A*S*H* fame), who is using the *Enterprise*'s photon technology to test his plan to reenergize his planet's fading sun.

They become close, but when the test fails, he must return to his planet; his sixtieth birthday is approaching, and death is compulsory at that age for everyone on that world. He is anguished, since his work must be continued by people who might need years to learn how to pick up where he left off.

Lwaxana convinces him that he doesn't have to follow tradition, and his decision to stay with her creates conflicts with his world, his family, and within himself. Ultimately, he decides to honor the traditions he was raised with and Lwaxana bravely decides to accompany him to his farewell ceremony.

"The Host," unknown to Beverly Crusher, is the body of her newfound lover Odan, an alien ambassador on a vital diplomatic mission that only he can carry off. Odan himself, however, is a parasitic being that uses the humanoid body as a vehicle.

When the body sickens and dies, the truth is revealed, and Beverly transfers Odan to the body of a volunteer—Riker—until a host from his home world can arrive. This is, of course, a great strain on Riker's body, as his personality is submerged beneath that of Odan—who still proclaims his love for Beverly.

She can't accept this turn of events and avoids Odan/Riker—until she can no longer reject him, and they embrace right before a strategically placed commercial break. Needless to say, the negotiations succeed and a host body arrives in time to save Riker. When it turns out to be a female body, Beverly must break off relations again, as all these body changes are beginning to bewilder her.

This is a very intelligent, well-done episode which seems to cop out at the end. Of course, it is understandable that the situation is stressful—but Beverly has already made love to Odan using Riker's body. And this is never touched upon later—wouldn't this be a violation of Riker's privacy? Does he ever find out? How does he feel about it? And the final rejection points up the fact that *Star Trek*'s morality is still seen through the veil of twentieth-century biases and opinions.

One interesting technical aspect of this episode, incidentally, is that it had to be shot in such a manner as to conceal the fact that Gates McFadden was pregnant.

"The Mind's Eye" has Geordi kidnapped by Romulans and brainwashed while an impostor takes his place at a conference. When he returns from his "vacation," he has false memories of a wonderful time—and a mission to kill a Klingon governor, part of a plot to undermine Klingon/Federation relations.

Fortunately, Data picks up the subspace transmissions controlling Geordi and manages to piece together the situation, stopping the assassination just in the nick of time. Data even narrows the choice of Geordi's controllers to two suspects: Picard or the Klingon ambassador Kell.

Picard gracefully offers to submit to a search for a personal subspace transmitter, but the Klingon unwisely refuses, and asks Picard for asylum when he realizes that he's sunk. Picard agrees to this request—but only after the other Klingons present have determined that the ambassador is, in fact, telling the truth.

This episode featured a brand-new, never-before-seen Romulan ship, which would appear once more in the season finale.

Astute listeners undoubtedly identified the voice of the Romulan mastermind lurking in the shadows during Geordi's brainwashing sequences—it was Denise Crosby.

"In Theory" details Data's first serious attempt at a romantic relationship when cadet Jenna falls for him on the rebound. Determined to discover the intricacies of human relationships, Data (remember, he's "fully functional") plunges into unchartered territories, certain that his maps (complete files on the literature of romance, among other things) will show him the way.

Unfortunately, it doesn't work out; Jenna herself is too immature to cut any slack for any of the vast gaps in Data's understanding. When the relationship goes sour, he begins to quote old movies and sitcoms—he even enters calling out "Honey, I'm home!"—which at least gives some insight into what remains of twentieth-century culture four centuries later.

A ship-threatening subplot detracts from the main story line, which is strangely disappointing for a Data-centered story. Brent Spiner is as good as usual, of course, and Michele Scarabelli is fine as the lovesick Jenna. First-time director Patrick Stewart does, at the least, an adequate job on this episode.

"Redemption" is finally made available to Worf, but under rather trying circumstances. Picard still can't shake his involvement in Klingon politics. As the official Arbiter of Succession, he must go to the Klingon home world to install Gowron as head of the High Council. Klingon politics are in a bit of turmoil; Duras's sisters, an unpleasant duo, have allegedly found Duras's son, a surly teen, and challenge Gowron's right. (They're also playing footsie with Romulans, including the one with the habit of remaining obscured by shadows.)

Worf's brother is part of a group of officers planning their own power play, but Worf throws in with Gowron and uses his seniority to pull his brother (and most of his brother's cohorts) over to his side. He does, however, wait until Gowron's back is against the wall—and he has a price. When Picard rejects the Duras family claim—their contender is young and unproven—the rest of the Council withdraws to the Duras camp at Gowron's accession, leaving the new ruler to restore Worf's family name alone.

Then, to avoid a conflict of interest, Worf resigns his Starfleet commission and joins with Gowron, and receives a touching send-off by the *Enterprise* crew. The ship then heads out of Klingon space, off to other missions . . .

. . . but down at the Duras family home, the shadowy Romulan leader steps into the light, revealing the familiar face of actress Denise Crosby, who had played Tasha Yar—and anticipating the return of Picard at some future date as well.

Although this lacks the heavy impact of "The Best of Both Worlds," it is a strong season ender, as Worf's departure is an emotional sequence, and his fate—along with that of Federation/Klingon relations—remains uncertain. Even the anticlimactic nature of his restoration of honor serves to underscore the perils that undoubtedly await him.

This is also counted as *The Next Generation*'s one hundredth episode by its producers, although to arrive at this figure one must count "Encounter at Farpoint" as two episodes. In fact, there is some justification for this, as it consisted of two unrelated scenarios slapped haphazardly together. One need only to have reflected on that ponderous pilot episode to have truly seen just how far *The Next Generation* had come since its inception.

CHAPTER ELEVEN

THE END OF A GENERATION

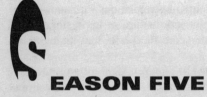

EASON FIVE

"Redemption, Part II," *The Next Generation*'s opener for season five, brings us back into the middle of the Klingon Civil War. On leave from the *Enterprise*, Worf and younger brother Kurn bring a critical number of Klingon ships to Gowron's aid, but the superior forces assembled by the Duras sisters are winning. If Gowron loses, with him go Worf's hopes of restoring his good name.

When the *Enterprise* finds evidence of the Duras family's traitorous dealings with the Romulans, it needs Starfleet's help to cut off their supply line, and Picard matches wits with Sela, Romulan daughter of Tasha Yar.

"Darmok" showcases Captain Picard's diplomatic skills when the *Enterprise* is sent to negotiate with the

Children of Tama, an inscrutable race with whom the Federation has always failed to communicate.

Picard is snatched from the *Enterprise* and marooned on a planet with the captain of the Tama ship. With his universal translator only picking up portions of his companion's speech, he hears only phrases such as "Darmok and Jalad at Tanagra." Picard discovers that the Children of Tama speak only in metaphors, describing their myths and historical past. He has been brought to the planet to replay the historical meeting of Darmok and Jalad, but must find his own ending to their story.

In "Ensign Ro," the Bajoran officer of that name has been transferred to the *Enterprise* to help it communicate with Bajoran terrorist Orta, accused of attacking a Federation colony.

When the *Enterprise* locates Orta and his gang, the crew discovers that the Bajoran could not possibly have attacked the distant Federation colony. With a clever ruse, the *Enterprise* tricks the Cardassians into attacking an empty Bajoran ship—and learns that the Cardassians had been behind the attack on the Federation.

The Crystalline Entity of "Datalore" returns in "Silicon Avatar," when Dr. Kila Marr joins the crew to seek out and study the destructive alien force that devours all living things. Marr's son was killed by the Entity on Omicron Theta, the deserted planet where Data was first discovered. At Marr's request, Data plays back her son's diary, which was loaded into Data's memory before the colony was destroyed.

Just as the *Enterprise* begins to communicate with the Crystalline Entity, Dr. Marr, more concerned with vengeance than with science or the discovery of new life, kills it.

In "Disaster," the *Enterprise* collides with a quantum filament, causing shipwide damage and isolating the bridge from the rest of the ship. The senior officers are scattered throughout the damaged ship, each heroically trying to do his duty, but not knowing what is happening elsewhere—or even if there are other survivors.

Picard, still not adjusted to having families on his ship, is trapped in a turbolift with three very young children and struggles to keep them calm by singing French folk songs while he tries to rescue them.

Worf, in charge of the wounded in Ten Forward, delivers botanist Keiko's baby.

Deanna, in command of the bridge, ignores Ensign Ro's advice to cut their losses and escape in the saucer section, gambling that someone in Engineering will prevent the warp core breach. Not surprisingly, the ship is saved, but each crew member must first take on some very uncharacteristic roles.

"The Game" is a headset Riker brings back from a holiday on Risa. The Game directly accesses the player's mind, and playing it gives intense physical pleasure. It is dangerously addictive, and only Wesley and the lovely young ensign Robin Lefler remain free of its control. Dr. Crusher shuts down Data, who is immune to the Game's attractions.

Wesley and friend reactivate Data, and together discover how to deprogram the crew. When aliens appear on the *Enterprise*'s bridge, and a brainwashed Picard seems about to hand over control, it is up to Wesley and Data to rescue the ship from treason.

In "Unification, Part I," the Federation sends Captain Picard to Vulcan to meet with Sarek, father of the legendary Spock. Spock has gone to Romulus without authorization, and is suspected of defecting to the enemy.

Dying of Bendii Syndrome, Sarek mind-melds with Picard before the Captain and Data head off to search for Spock.

"Unification, Part II" reveals that Spock is working with an underground group that seeks to reunify Vulcan and Romulus. Disguised as Romulans, Picard and Data locate Spock, who insists that this is not Federation business, but a personal peace mission.

Sarek dies, and Picard relates to Spock his father's very human feelings for his legendary son.

Sela, Tasha Yar's Romulan daughter, gets involved, and it turns out that this "unification" is actually a Romulan plot to merge with Vulcan, on Romulan terms. Nevertheless, Spock's presence has encouraged some very real resistance to the totalitarian Romulan government, which it now appears may someday be overthrown.

A visitor from the future appears in "A Matter of Time," declaring that he is on the *Enterprise* to view an unspecified series of important events. Dr. Rasmussen, it turns out, is a figure from the past, not the future, and his errand is much darker than mere study.

This part was originally written for Robin Williams, a longtime *Trek* fan who wanted to appear on the show, but when the actor was unavailable the role was taken over by Matt Frewer.

"New Ground" has the *Enterprise* testing the Soliton Wave, a revolutionary propulsion system that will far outstrip warp 10. Dr. Ja'Dar joins the ship at Lemma II to begin the experiment with the wave. When the technology works too well, but is uncontrollable, Data and Geordi struggle to find a way to stop it from destroying Lemma II.

Meanwhile, Worf's son Alexander has proved to be a handful for Worf's human parents, and Alexander joins his father on the *Enterprise*. Worf, with Deanna's help, begins to learn parenting skills, but must also keep up his duties as chief of security.

Patrick Stewart directs "Hero Worship," where an away team investigating the damaged exploratory vessel *Vico* discovers that the only survivor is a young boy. Convinced that he himself is somehow responsible for the deaths of his parents and the rest of the *Vico*'s crew, Timothy begins to idolize Data and to imitate the android. Since he wants to be more human, Data is puzzled by a human who wants to be a machine, but becomes friends with the troubled boy and helps him to overcome his grief and appreciate his own humanity.

The *Enterprise* initially welcomes the Ullian telepaths on board in "Violations," but fun and games dissolve into threat when someone begins entering and raping the minds of Riker, Troi, and Dr. Crusher. The Ullians deny the violation, and Picard must use all his diplomatic skills to discover the true culprit.

"The Masterpiece Society" of Moab IV is endangered when a stellar core fragment heads for their planet. The *Enterprise* visits this old Federation colony, sealed off from outside contact for more than two hundred years, in an effort to rescue the inhabitants. Like all utopias, Moab IV has a dark side: its discontented youths seek to escape from the strict regime aboard the *Enterprise*, and Picard must wrestle with his conscience to decide their fate.

The *Enterprise* is scanned by a small vessel in "Conundrum," and everyone on board loses his or her memory. The computer tells them they are at war, with a mission to destroy enemy ships and outposts. The *Enterprise* destroys several ships on behalf of their allies, the Lysians, but the crew begins to suspect there might be something wrong. No one recognizes the warlike new bridge officer, and oddly the Sartarran enemy is no match for a Galaxy-class starship.

It turns out that the Lysians, tired of a long war with the Sartarrans, took over the *Enterprise* to dupe it into obliterating their enemies. Picard recovers in time to see what he has done—but is it in time to stop the war?

In "Power Play," Troi, Data, and O'Brien become possessed by hostile alien entities shortly after beaming down to an uninhabited moon. With the aliens controlling their bodies, the officers hijack Ten Forward and hold the patrons prisoner. Troi claims to be Captain Bryce Shumar of the starship *Essex*, trying to get his crew's remains back home. However, the aliens are really the leaders of a group of five hundred criminals, existing only as consciousnesses and exiled long ago to this moon as punishment for their crimes.

Worf's spine is severed in a terrible accident in "Ethics," and he learns he will be permanently disabled. As a Klingon, Worf considers this worse than dying, and requests Riker's aid in a ritual suicide, throwing the first officer into a quandary over whether he can assist in a friend's death, however honorable that death. Worf must also face his son Alexander, who sees he is about to lose his one remaining parent.

Dr. Crusher, trying to understand the Klingon code, encourages Worf to go on living. A visiting doctor, Toby Russell, wants to try an experimental technique that will clone Worf's spine, enabling Dr. Crusher to heal him completely. At Worf's request, the cloning and surgery are performed, but Worf dies on the operating table.

At the last moment, however, Worf resurrects, and Dr. Crusher discovers that the unique redundancy of Klingon anatomy enabled Worf to survive the surgery and only appear to be dead. Father and son are reconciled, and it seems that Worf will make a complete recovery.

"The Outcast" is Soren, a member of the J'naii, an androgynous race, with whom Riker falls in love. The *Enterprise* has been asked to assist the J'naii in locating a missing shuttlecraft, and Riker gets close to Soren, who becomes more and more feminine through contact with him. "She" begins to return his sexual interest.

The J'naii, in a long-ago quest for equality, outlawed gender differences, and to exhibit the traits of one sex or the other is considered a crime. Soren is seized and taken away to be "corrected," in spite of Riker's protests on "her" behalf.

Jonathan Frakes directed "Cause and Effect," a heart-stopping time-travel episode where the *Enterprise* is destroyed again and again at the end of an endlessly repeated day.

Riker, Worf, Dr. Crusher, and Data open the episode with a poker game, and the entire crew experiences déjà vu throughout the day. Another ship appears on the viewscreen, collision is imminent, and Captain Picard cries "Abandon ship!" just before the *Enterprise* explodes. After a commercial break, the scene returns to the poker game, the déjà vu, and the excruciating destruction of the *Enterprise*, twice more. When Dr. Crusher manages to record the mysterious voices she hears in her room, the crew learns that they are in a time loop that leads to their destruction. But knowledge is not necessarily power, and the crew must discover how to stop the vicious cycle.

Kelsey Grammer has a cameo as the captain of another Starfleet vessel, caught in the time loop for more than eighty years and finally returned to real time by the *Enterprise*.

"The First Duty" shows a less-than-perfect Wesley Crusher. Captain Picard and Dr. Crusher visit Starfleet Academy, where Wesley was slightly injured in a flight accident. Another of his squadron was killed in the incident, and the leader of Nova Squadron wants Wesley to help him blame the dead cadet for the accident—and cover up the squadron's illegal maneuver.

When the academy's investigation gets too close, the Nova Squadron survivors must decide whether to risk their careers and come clean or to allow their dead friend to bear the dishonor.

"Cost of Living" explores the family struggles of Worf and Deanna. While the engineering crew is busy trying to save the *Enterprise* from mysterious parasites, Worf must come to grips with Alexander's bad behavior. Deanna's mother, Lwaxana Troi, is on board, and wishes Captain Picard to perform a marriage ceremony between herself and a very staid, ritual-conscious man she's never met.

Lwaxana escapes her troubles by bringing Alexander to the holodeck, where they enjoy laughter and mud baths, to the dismay of both Worf and Deanna. To her groom's horror, Lwaxana then bares her true self, attending her wedding in traditional Betazoid style—stark naked.

"The Perfect Mate" is the solution two long-warring societies have decided will finally end their strife. The *Enterprise* agrees to deliver the Kriosians' peace offering to Valt Minor, and stores the mysterious canister in the cargo bay.

When two Ferengi passengers try to steal the cargo, they accidentally deactivate the stasis field and release the Kriosian peace offering—Kamala, a beautiful woman bred to be the perfect mate to the first man she meets. In this case, that man is an intrigued, but reluctant, Captain Picard.

Picard is appalled at Kamala's involuntary slavery, and at the same time is very attracted to the woman who has metamorphosed into his perfect mate.

Kamala decides to continue to Valt Minor, but her encounter with Picard has changed her into an independent, free-thinking woman, not just the perfect helpmeet she was intended to be.

A young girl is the center of attention in "Imaginary Friend," when Clara Sutter tells Counselor Troi about Isabella, her imaginary best friend. Clara's normal childhood fantasy takes a strange twist when the *Enterprise* enters a nebula and an alien comes on board and brings Isabella to life. But the girls' friendship turns sour, as Isabella deliberately causes freak accidents on board the ship.

Counselor Troi learns that the alien chose the form of a child to study humans through how they treat their young, and that the accidents were a result of the alien's confusion about parent-child relationships. In a predictably happy ending, Troi and Clara persuade the alien to depart.

The *Enterprise* investigates a Borg crash site in "I, Borg," and Dr. Crusher, against Picard's orders, insists on rescuing the only survivor.

Cut off from the collective, the male Borg seems less threatening, and Geordi and Dr. Crusher befriend him as he recovers. Geordi introduces the basic human concept of selfhood, and gives the Borg a name, Hugh. The Borg becomes less machine, more person, through his contact with the humans.

Picard has agreed to accept the Borg on board only as long as they can gain useful information from him. When Data programs a virus for Hugh to transmit to the Borg collective, Picard's personal loathing of the Borg is at war with Beverly's and Geordi's eloquent pleas against xenocide.

In "The Next Phase," Geordi and Ensign Ro are killed in a transporter accident—or so it seems to their crewmates. Actually, the two officers are alive and on board, but intangible and invisible to everyone but each other.

When their strange situation enables them to overhear a Romulan plot to sabotage the *Enterprise* and keep secret the new interphase generator, Geordi and Ro must find a way to save the ship, and get themselves, alive, back into their proper place.

"The Inner Light" showcases Patrick Stewart's versatile acting. An alien probe renders the captain unconscious on the bridge, and while his crew try to awaken him, Picard relives the memories of Kamin, the man who sent the probe before his planet's sun went supernova.

As Kamin, Picard experiences the family pleasures of a wife, children, and good friends in a small village. Yet he retains a puzzling memory of having been a starship captain, and still dreams of space travel. When the planet's sun grows too strong, the aging Kamin persuades his people to launch a space probe so that their history and way of life will not be lost.

When Picard comes to on the bridge, he is torn by relief and grief. His one souvenir is the wooden flute Kamin played, left in his possession by the probe. Throughout the next seasons, Picard plays this instrument in his quiet and thoughtful moments.

Kamin's young son Batai is played by Daniel Stewart, Patrick Stewart's real-life son.

This episode won the 1993 Hugo Award for Best Dramatic Presentation from the World Science Fiction Society.

For the season finale, the *Enterprise* begins a journey back in time to nineteenth-century San Francisco. In "Time's Arrow, Part I," Data's severed head is discovered in an excavation beneath the old city, but no one knows how it could have gotten there, until an investigation of strange energy readings leads the android across a portal that takes him through both time and space.

Trapped in old-time California, Data explains his strangeness by telling people he is from Brazil. Setting himself up as a cardplayer and scientist, he uses his poker winnings to purchase materials to make a transmitter to try to contact the *Enterprise*.

Data meets an unexpected friend in San Francisco, but the show—and the season—ends before we learn what Guinan is doing on nineteenth-century Earth.

SEASON SIX

"Time's Arrow, Part II" opens season six, and brings Captain Picard, Riker, Dr. Crusher, and Geordi, complete with period costumes, to old-time San Francisco in search of their missing crewmate.

The author Samuel Clemens—pen name Mark Twain—is suspicious of both Data and Guinan, and the *Enterprise* crew must solve the mystery that brought them there, and get out of town, without letting him discover their true origins. The "real" aliens turn out to be beings who take human shape and steal the souls of derelicts and drunks, transporting them back to an asteroid for food. The *Enterprise* must save humanity from being devoured, one by one, and rescue Data from the accident that destroyed him and left his head to be found beneath the city five hundred years later.

"Realm of Fear" centers on the transporter phobia of Lieutenant Barclay (Dwight Schultz). A highly intelligent engineer, Barclay—like Dr. McCoy and Dr. Pulaski before him—seems to harbor an unreasonable fear of the transporter. This time, however, his fear is well-founded, and the strange creatures he sees swimming in the beam pose a very real threat to the *Enterprise*—and explain the mystery of the abandoned ship the crew has found float-ing in space.

In "Man of the People," the *Enterprise* answers a dis-tress call near Rekag-Seronia, a planet at war with the neighboring Circoneans. Aboard the threatened ship is Ves Alkar, a Lumerian ambassador en route to the planet to help resolve the conflict.

Ves Alkar's diplomacy is unusual, and when he uses Counselor Troi as a dumping ground for his negative emotions, Deanna's personality changes dramatically, for the worse. The *Enterprise* must cope with two con-flicts: the war on Rekag-Seronia, and a ship's coun-selor who has been co-opted by a malevolent alien consciousness.

"Relics" joins the engineering skills of two *Star Trek* generations, when the *Enterprise* rescues Lieutenant

Commander Montgomery Scott (reprised by James Doohan) from a seventy-five-year-old shipwreck.

The *Enterprise* is exploring the Dyson sphere, an artificial structure built around a G-type star to form a unique solar system. Scotty's ship, the *Jenolan*, crashed outside the sphere years ago, when Scotty was on his way to a retirement colony. The wily engineer used the transporter to put himself in stasis.

When the *Enterprise* is trapped in the Dyson sphere, Scotty and Geordi, on board the wrecked *Jenolan*, must blend their very different—and sometimes conflicting—engineering styles to free the ship.

"Schisms" presents a mystery for the *Enterprise* to unravel when crew members, including Riker and Worf, exhibit symptoms of fatigue and unusual phobias. When an exhausted Riker sleeps through his alarm, he reports to sick bay. Dr. Crusher finds nothing wrong with him—except that his arm has been severed, and reattached.

Crew members are being stolen from the ship in their sleep and returned with no conscious memory of their experiences. Worf, Geordi, and other kidnapping victims assemble on the holodeck, using its equipment to trigger memories of the experiments and tortures they underwent. But understanding the danger is not enough, and the *Enterprise* must move quickly before another crewmate dies.

Student intern Amanda Rogers joins the *Enterprise* in "True Q." Amanda is set to spend her time on board learning about starships and Starfleet, and doing research. When Q appears and draws out her long-subdued powers, her life changes dramatically. While Q and Amanda play a game of hide-and-seek, from the cargo bay to the warp core, Picard and Data investigate the true fate of Amanda's parents, victims of a freak weather accident on Earth.

Amanda learns that her parents had been Q, living as

humans and executed by the Q Continuum for their rebellion. Suddenly, these powers are not all fun and games, and Amanda must choose between being Q and being fully human.

The next generation boards the *Enterprise*, this time from behind the scenes as Adam Nimoy, Leonard's son, directs his first episode, "Rascals."

Returning from shore leave, Captain Picard, Guinan, Ensign Ro, and Keiko O'Brien are nearly torn to pieces with their shuttle as it passes through an unusual cloud formation. Interference from the cloud affects their bodies, and when they transport to the *Enterprise* they begin to age—backward.

There is no time to return the victims to normal before Captain Picard, now an adult in an adolescent's body, must stave off a Ferengi invasion of his ship.

A layover at a starbase gives Geordi and Data the opportunity to experiment with the android's positronic brain in "A Fistful of Datas." Geordi links his friend to the computer net.

Worf, joining his son Alexander on the holodeck, plays the sheriff in a rough town from the American Old West. Alexander's game turns dangerous when he is kidnapped, and all the villains look like . . . Data, complete with the android's superhuman strength and intelligence. Unable to stop the program, Worf on the holodeck, and Geordi in Engineering, must find separate ways to stop Data and rescue Alexander. Patrick Stewart directed this episode.

Jonathan Frakes directed "The Quality of Life," in which Picard must decide what constitutes life in a situation where Starfleet has a great deal invested in a negative answer.

Geordi and Data visit Tyrus, an important research site, where a particle fountain is scheduled to provide a new energy source. Unstable and behind schedule, the project can only be saved by "exocomps," intelligent robots designed to diagnose and correct problems within the particle fountain. Their creator, Dr. Farallon, may have made them too intelligent, and the exocomps begin to exhibit signs of self-preservation. Data, taking at face value the definition of life, insists the robots are sentient, living creatures. When Data refuses to allow the exocomps to annihilate themselves while working on the particle fountain, both the Tyran project and the Federation's definition of life hang in the balance.

In "Chain of Command, Part I," Picard is relieved of his command by Vice Admiral Nechayev. On a mission of deepest secrecy, he is sent to Celtris III with Dr. Crusher and Worf to check out rumors of a Cardassian base and a possible assault on the Federation. The officers walk into a trap and Picard is captured, not knowing that Dr. Crusher and Worf have escaped.

Beverly and Worf return to the *Enterprise*, but Picard is considered dead.

"Chain of Command, Part II" accelerates the pace, with the *Enterprise* facing off against a Cardassian threat. Riker, convinced Picard is alive, is relieved of his duties when he agitates too strongly for a rescue mission.

Picard's captor, Gul Madred, tortures the captain in an attempt to force him to reveal Federation secrets. The sadistic Cardassian turns the examination into a game of willpower, seeking to break Picard for his own amusement.

While the *Enterprise* stares down the Cardassians, demanding the return of her captain, Picard is alone with his captor, struggling simply to maintain his identity and integrity.

"Ship in a Bottle" explores the nature of holodeck characters, and their possible powers. Lieutenant Barclay, investigating a malfunction on the holodeck, discovers a file in which Sherlock Holmes's nemesis, Professor

Moriarty, has achieved consciousness. True to his character, Moriarty succeeds in taking control of the *Enterprise*, holding it hostage in exchange for a release from his limited existence. With Moriarty in control, however, the *Enterprise* comes dangerously close to a star about to go nova.

In his efforts to placate Moriarty, Data finds clues about how the villain originally gained control of the ship, and begins searching for a solution that will guarantee the real *Enterprise*, and the fictional Moriarty, continued life.

Geordi begins to fall in love with "Aquiel," a Starfleet officer posted at a subspace relay station and suspected of killing her superior officer. When the *Enterprise* makes a routine stop at the station, its crew finds evidence of a murder, but only a dog alive. Browsing the journals of Lieutenant Aquiel Uhnari, Geordi becomes convinced that she cannot have killed Lieutenant Keith Rocha, though the provocation was strong. When the missing Uhnari is picked up by the Klingons and brought to the *Enterprise*, the mystery deepens. Having lost his heart, Geordi nearly loses his life before finding the murderer.

"Face of the Enemy" presents Counselor Troi in the unusual guise of a Romulan. When Troi, returning to the *Enterprise* after a conference, awakens from sleeping, she discovers that she has been surgically altered and is on board a Romulan ship.

Subcommander N'Vek introduces her to the crew of the *Khazara* as Rakal, a high-ranking officer for the Romulan intelligence service, the Tal Shiar. With almost no information, and less choice, Troi commandeers the *Khazara*, overrides the orders of the ship's captain, and heads for Federation space. In a mission far removed from her usual "Captain, I sense. . . ," Troi must smuggle three members of the Romulan underground to safety, and find a way to return home herself.

"Welcome to the afterlife, Jean-Luc. You're dead," announces Q at the beginning of "Tapestry." Injured on an away team, Picard is in sick bay, dying in spite of Dr. Crusher's expertise. The omnipotent Q seizes Picard's trauma as an excuse to play with the human psyche, forcing Picard to relive critical moments in his life.

Q learns of young Picard's fight with the Nausicaans, which resulted in his artificial heart. Offering to change history, Q shows Picard the very different self he might have been had he walked away from that fight. This alternate Picard is not dying in the *Enterprise*'s sick bay, but is very much alive and well. Offered the opportunity to change his life—and thereby avert his death—Captain Picard refuses to accept Q's bargain, and awakens instead on Beverly's operating table, laughing.

"Birthright, Part I" brings the *Enterprise* to Deep Space Nine, where the starship is to give technical assistance to nearby Bajor. Aboard the station, Worf encounters someone who says that Worf's father survived the Khitomer massacre, and may be alive. Worf travels to the Romulan planet where the survivors are said to be held captive, and finds Klingons, but the situation is slightly different from what he expected.

Back on the *Enterprise*, Data is injured in an accident, and while "unconscious" begins hallucinating about Dr. Soong. Dr. Bashir, of DS 9, guesses that Data has been dreaming, and Data begins a quest to explore this possibility.

Imprisoned by his own people in "Birthright, Part II," Worf discovers that the Klingons in the Romulan compound are indeed survivors of Khitomer, but have no wish to rejoin the Klingon Empire. Shamed at having survived the massacre and fallen into Romulan hands, the elders prefer to be thought dead. Worf is shocked at how little the youths know of their own culture, and by teaching ancient Klingon ways begins to persuade some of the community to join him in escaping.

Meanwhile, Data is able to return to his dream state, once again envisioning Dr. Soong, and learning more about the plans his "father" has for him.

At the beginning of "Starship Mine," Captain Picard, forced to leave his ship while it undergoes baryon radiation cleaning, has little on his mind except horses. Attending a boring diplomatic cocktail party with his crew, Picard escapes back to the ship to retrieve his saddle, only to discover that the starbase cleaning team is more than it seems. Playing cat and mouse with terrorists, trying to keep one step ahead of the radiation sweep, Picard fights for command of his ship, and his own survival.

On the starbase, the cocktail party has turned into a hostage situation. Riker, Deanna, Dr. Crusher, Data, and Geordi must use their wits, and Geordi's visor, to free themselves and find Picard.

"Lessons" gives Captain Picard an unusual role, that of romantic hero. A night-watch conversation with Lieutenant Commander Neela Daren reveals that the two share a deep love of music, and much more.

As the captain comes to grips with new personal and professional conflicts, he must send Daren on a dangerous mission to evacuate an endangered outpost. Massive storms threaten the away team, and Daren is presumed dead when she does not return. Troubled by her loss, and by the fact that he sent her to her death, Picard has a violent introduction to romance with a crew member. When Daren finally reappears, she and Picard must find a solution that allows them to pursue their careers and to find some measure of happiness together.

"The Chase," directed by Jonathan Frakes, is a galactic treasure hunt that even duty-bound Captain Picard cannot resist. His old mentor, archaeologist Professor Richard Galen, comes on board the *Enterprise* and asks Picard to join him in a great project. Picard refuses, but when Galen dies in an attack on his shuttle, the *Enterprise* drops everything and follows Galen's clues to a distant planet.

On the planet, the away team encounters Romulans, Klingons, and Ferengi, all looking for the final piece to the ancient puzzle. Only Picard's diplomatic skills keep the races from killing one another before the final puzzle is solved and they hear a remarkable message from a long-dead ancestor.

Rehearsals for Dr. Crusher's play have a strange effect on Riker in "Frame of Mind." Dr. Crusher's play is about a madman and his doctor, and Riker seems to phase from playing a madman to being an inmate in an asylum.

Imprisoned in the asylum, Riker is told that his life in Starfleet is a hallucination and that he is seriously ill. The first officer must pierce through multiple levels of consciousness and various roles. Starfleet officer, actor in a play, madman—before finally coming to the dark reality that he has been kidnapped and held prisoner for an unknown reason, and with no way to escape.

Dr. Crusher's ethics are questioned in "Suspicions," when she is relieved of duty for performing an illegal autopsy on a dead Ferengi. As she packs for her return to Earth for trial, Beverly relays to Guinan the events leading up to the death, and her subsequent actions.

Dr. Crusher was hosting a small conference for scientists to test "metaphasic shielding," which would allow a vessel to penetrate a star's corona. Tempers, and rivalries, ran high among her guests, and as Dr. Crusher unravels her story, she remains convinced that the Ferengi scientist was murdered. Dr. Crusher is proved right, but only when her shuttle is hijacked by Dr. Jo'Bril, who confesses his crime and now threatens Beverly as well.

An ancient Klingon hero comes to life in "Rightful Heir." Worf, on leave from the *Enterprise* to pursue a spiritual quest, is meditating on the planet Boreth in a temple honoring the legendary Kahless, the Klingon "once and future king" who promised to return to lead his people. Worf's vision of the hero takes on a very real existence, throwing the Klingon Empire into turmoil.

Worf brings Kahless to the *Enterprise* to meet with Gowron, who is skeptical at this challenge to his leadership. Dr. Crusher's DNA tests show that Kahless is indeed the incarnation of the ancient hero, but his method of coming to the twenty-fourth century is as dramatic as his appearance itself, and will have a profound effect on his role in the empire.

LeVar Burton debuted as a director with "Second Chances." The *Enterprise* is at Nervala IV to recover scientific data left there eight years before, when Commander Riker evacuated the planet while serving on another ship.

Commander Riker finds an unexpected inhabitant of the installation—another Riker, who has been trapped alone for eight years after a transporter accident left him on the planet. In reality, the transporter divided Riker, leaving one version to continue his career and the other to continue, alone, in a desperate situation.

Lieutenant Riker, aboard the *Enterprise* for the first time, wants to pick up his interrupted relationship with Deanna, who is charmed by advances from a Riker who is willing to put his love for her before his career. Commander Riker, coping with the retrieval mission, discovers he needs his "other self," and the two reach an uneasy truce. Lieutenant Riker, who decides to call himself by his middle name, Thomas, is not so different from Picard's Number One: he decides to leave Deanna and jump-start what will prove to be a very interesting Starfleet career.

"Timescape" opens on a shuttlecraft, where Picard, Data, Geordi, and Troi are returning to the *Enterprise* after a conference. They begin to experience moments of frozen or accelerated time, which seem small problems compared to what they find back at the ship.

The *Enterprise* is frozen in time, in combat with a Romulan ship. On board, the crew is also frozen, with a warp core breach in progress. On the Romulan ship, there is evidence of an evacuation to the *Enterprise* and of mysterious aliens in the drive system that may hold the clues to the situation. Using portable devices that allow them to move freely in the frozen scene, Geordi, Data, and Troi must unravel the events that led to the conflict and find a way to restart normal time without destroying both ships.

"Descent, Part I" closes the sixth season. The scene opens on the holodeck, where Data is in conversation with Sir Isaac Newton, Albert Einstein, and quantum physicist Stephen Hawking—played by the man himself.

The story gets moving when the *Enterprise* answers a distress call from the Federation outpost on Ohniaka III, only to discover that the Borg have been there first. But the Borg are behaving strangely, murdering the outpost crew rather than assimilating them. While fighting off another Borg attack, Data experiences his first emotion— anger. Before he can come to terms with this negative emotion, he is kidnapped. At the close of the episode, Data joins his brother Lore in command of a group of rebel Borg.

East Coast Trekkers will remember this episode, less for its moderately suspenseful ending than for the fact that the broadcast was preempted midway by news coverage of U.S. air strikes against Iraq.

SEASON SEVEN

In "Descent, Part II," Lore has his brother Data literally under his thumb, by means of a controller chip, embedded in his thumbnail, that gives Data the one drug he cannot resist: emotion.

Lore is in command of a splinter group of Borg, intent on leading them against the Federation. In the eyes of the Borg, Lore and Data are gods, the sentient robots the Borg themselves aspire to be.

The *Enterprise* away team encounters Hugh (from "I, Borg") and attempts to persuade him to join them in resisting Lore. Picard is captured by Lore's minions. When Lore decides to test his brother's loyalty by asking him to murder his former captain, the fate of Picard—and the Federation—hangs in the balance.

Captain Picard barely survives a shuttle crash on a planetoid in "Liaisons." He is rescued by the only inhabitant, a woman stranded there many years ago and living in the relic of her vessel. She seems happy to nurse him back to health, and glad of the company—perhaps too glad. When Picard makes plans to leave, her true nature reveals itself, and threatens the captain as effectively as the original crash.

"Interface" introduces a new "virtual reality" technology, with its own very real dangers. The *Enterprise* answers a distress call from the U.S.S. *Raman*, trapped in the atmosphere of a gas giant. During the rescue mission, Geordi gets word that his mother's ship, the U.S.S. *Hera*, is missing and presumed lost. Despite conversations with his father (played by Ben Vereen), Geordi is in denial, convinced his mother will somehow return.

Using a direct neural interface with an *Enterprise* probe, Geordi communicates with the *Raman*, only to discover the crew is dead. During a later VR session, while exploring the fate of the *Raman*, Geordi sees his mother in the control room of the disabled ship, urgently pleading with him to come down to the planet. Disobeying a direct order, Geordi, accompanied by Data, heads for the planet, determined to rescue his mother—at all costs.

Captain Picard disappears in "Gambit I," and Riker must go undercover to try to locate him. He, Dr. Crusher, and Worf pose as galactic travelers, tough-talking, tough-acting, and very, very determined to get information. One scene in a crowded bar has echoes of a very famous canteen from *Star Wars*.

Picard resurfaces in "Gambit II," using the name Galen and posing as an archaeologist. He has uncovered a team of pirates who are plundering ancient Vulcan sights and stealing artifacts. While the pirates are in it for the money, Picard is far more interested in their sponsors—the Romulans.

The crew is literally eaten alive in "Phantasms," when warp core repairs at a starbase seem to backfire. Data has been dreaming again, this time of a party in Ten Forward, where Deanna is served as cake! Peptic celluloid cake, "with mint icing," says Worf.

When Data's dreams reveal that the crew are being drained of their life force by parasites visible only to him, it is a race against time to discover the cure before the parasites devour the crew, and the ship.

A brief encounter on the *Enterprise* sends Deanna's mother into a coma in "Dark Page," and a reluctant Troi must mind-link with her parent to determine the cause. One of the strongest of Betazoid telepaths, Lwaxana resists Deanna's intrusions for a long time, and the counselor despairs of saving her mother from a self-willed death. At last, Deanna gains entry into one of her mother's oldest memories, and learns of a sister she never knew she had—a sister whose fate will result in either Lwaxana's rescue or her death.

Captain Picard and Dr. Crusher are kidnapped while beaming down to a warring planet in "Attached," directed by Jonathan Frakes. Invited to the planet by one of the factions seeking entrance to the Federation, the *Enterprise* tries to determine the nation's preparedness for citizenship.

Convinced that Picard and Crusher are spies for their enemies, the other nation, the Kez, kidnaps them and implants devices designed to drain their minds of information. With help from the underground rebellion, Picard and Crusher escape, determining to make their way on foot to the border.

While Riker argues with both sides to get Picard and Crusher released, the two escapees discover that the devices implanted in their brains enable them to read each other's thoughts. As the two old friends make their way to safety, they begin together a stranger journey into each other's thoughts, feelings, and long-suppressed passions.

"Force of Nature" seems to spell doom for space travel as the Federation knows it. Researchers from a planet too near a major "thruway" have discovered that the passage of ships at high warp has been destroying their system, and insist that no vessel travel faster than warp 6, ever.

Picard wants to be skeptical of their findings, but his own crew verify the researchers' data, and he knows his actions will determine the nature of space travel for the rest of the Federation.

Data's family continues to grow, and in "Inheritance" he meets his "mother," the woman who assisted Dr. Soong in his creation. Data is intrigued, and pleased, to claim this highly intelligent, charming woman as his family. But she is not entirely what she seems, and Data learns a secret about his mother that even she does not know—and must make a life-or-death decision for her.

In "Parallels," Worf returns victorious from a bat'telh tournament, but soon discovers that the *Enterprise* is not quite the ship he left. To begin with, his tournament trophy suddenly becomes a second-place award, as he lost to a player using illegal moves. Then, Deanna breezes into his quarters, and apparently she is his wife.

As events go more askew, only Worf understands that

the reality he has encountered is parallel to, but not exactly like, that on the *Enterprise* he knows. Finding a way to get back across a sea of possible universes is as great a challenge as the bat'telh, with more profound repercussions.

LeVar Burton directs "The Pegasus," which opens with a visit from Riker's former captain, Admiral Pressman. Pressman has changed since Riker knew him, however, and seems to have some highly secret, and highly unusual, plans for the Federation.

The two come to fisticuffs, and Pressman's superhuman strength clues Riker into the fact that the admiral is more than he seems. Admiral Pressman has voluntarily joined with an insectlike life-form, and plans to transform the Federation with the aliens' help. His intended first convert: Commander Riker.

"Homeward" introduces Worf's foster brother, and casts the Klingon into a moral dilemma. His brother asks for the *Enterprise*'s aid to create a new atmosphere for his dying adopted planet. Unfortunately, the inhabitants, who think the human is one of them, are an extremely ethnocentric people, convinced they are the center of the universe. They have little technology. Following the Prime Directive, even though it means the loss of an entire people, Picard refuses to help.

Not unlike Worf, his brother takes matters into his own hands, and beams his people aboard the *Enterprise*, without their knowledge. An incensed Picard must either rescue the citizens or return them to certain death.

"Sub Rosa" uncovers deep secrets at the heart of Dr. Crusher's family. Lingering on Arvada III after her grandmother's funeral, Dr. Crusher begins reading her nana's diaries, and learns of a secret, lifelong lover. Despite mysterious warnings from a neighbor, Beverly continues her research into her grandmother's life, and is soon visited herself by a ghostly, but ardent, lover.

The *Enterprise* is in orbit to assist the colony's weather scientists, and Deanna and Picard grow uneasy about Beverly's new obsession. When the doctor resigns and prepares to remain on Arvada III, Picard forces a confrontation with the demon lover, and begins a struggle for Beverly's life and soul. Jonathan Frakes directed this very creepy episode.

"Lower Decks" concentrates on the worries and ambitions of a group of junior officers. Like their superiors, they play poker and use the time to discuss their hopes and dreams. Someone is due for a promotion to the operations position on the bridge, and the rivalry is friendly, but intense.

The officers are severely tested when a Cardassian, spying for the Federation, boards the ship, and the *Enterprise* must return him to his own people under deep cover. Bajoran Ensign Sito joined the *Enterprise* in spite of her smudged record at Starfleet Academy, where she had been a member of Wesley's Nova Squadron, from "The First Duty." Picard gives her the chance to prove herself, and sends her undercover, disguised as the Cardassian's "prisoner." The outcome of this mission will determine who gets the Ops position, but the junior officers may not be pleased with the decision.

Data suffers amnesia in "Thine Own Self," and is marooned on a primitive planet after investigating a highly dangerous ship crash site. Wandering into a village with only a strangely marked metal case, Data is befriended by the natives, and is willing to make a life among them. A local metalworker uses materials from Data's case to make some striking jewelry, and Data begins to feel at home.

The villagers soon begin to sicken and die, however, and when they decide that Data is the cause of the illness, the *Enterprise* must move quickly to save him from their wrath.

An alien probe begins to take over the *Enterprise* in "Masks," transforming it—and Commander Data—into the elements of an ancient mythos. As the ship devolves into jungle and stone, only Data holds the clues to solving the riddle. Possessed by the personalities of dead gods, Data alternates between their personalities, reluctantly providing Captain Picard with information about an age-old conflict. Using the holodeck to re-create an ancient temple of the sun, Picard unleashes the gods, and the outcome of their battle will decide the fate of the *Enterprise*.

"Eye of the Beholder" has Deanna seeing ghosts. During a visit to one of the nacelles to investigate a crew member's suicide, Troi picks up residues of fear and horror that date back to the building of the ship itself. As she unravels a seven-year-old murder mystery, the Betazoid becomes lost in the past. Involved in the victim's emotions, including an uncontrolled jealousy that has her convinced Worf is cheating on her, Deanna struggles to solve the murder. But in doing so, she must untangle her life from a dangerous pattern of jealousy, murder, and suicide.

Gates McFadden directed her first episode with "Genesis." Returning to the *Enterprise* after a short trip, Captain Picard and Commander Data find the crew transformed into strange and dangerous creatures. It seems they have "de-evolved," resorting to ancestral life-forms. Riker has become an ape, and a wildly dangerous proto-Klingon is on the loose and mad with lust for Deanna, now amphibious. Endangered by a rampaging Worf, Picard and Data must rescue the ship, and recover the crew, before Picard himself succumbs to the deadly virus.

"Journey's End" brings back Wesley Crusher, now an Academy graduate posted to the *Enterprise*. Wesley has changed from the eager-to-please whiz kid of earlier seasons, and neither Dr. Crusher nor Captain Picard can get through to the young man.

The *Enterprise* is on a mission to evacuate a colony of Native Americans from a planet ceded to the Cardassians. Under the guidance of the tribe, Wesley begins a spiritual quest. The Traveler ("Time Squared," Season two) returns and invites Wesley to join him and explore space and time in a whole new way. The rest of the crew is left to face recalcitrant colonists and warlike Cardassians in the less-than-glamorous real world.

Worf and his son Alexander visit a distant Klingon outpost in "Firstborn." At a marketplace fighting exhibition, Worf demonstrates basic Klingon skills to a reluctant Alexander. Worf is horrified that his son has no wish to be a warrior, and only the intervention of a mysterious stranger can begin to reconcile the equally stubborn father and son.

"Bloodlines" continues to explore the father-son theme, this time introducing an unknown, and unexpected, offspring for Captain Picard. The teenager cares nothing for a father he never knew he had, despite Picard's overtures to the boy. A troublemaker on his home planet, the teenager's DNA tests reveal that he is not a Picard after all.

The captain's Ferengi nemesis, Bok, remains convinced Picard was responsible for the death of his own son, and wants to get back at Picard by killing the boy. Picard has a great deal of trouble protecting a "son" who wants no part of him whatsoever.

The holodeck begins to take over the ship in "Emergence." Command functions are routed to the holodeck, which is running an unusual program of a speeding train, Old West style. Clues to the ship's purpose can only be gained from the obscure statements of holodeck characters. Out of the crew's control, the *Enterprise* heads for a nebula, where Data and Geordi finally discover that the vessel is in search of omicron particles, a critical energy source.

Finally accessing sufficient energy, the ship "gives birth" in the cargo bay to a strange and beautiful new life-form. The episode ends, but the mystery is far from solved.

Patrick Stewart directed the final regular-season episode, "Preemptive Strike." Ensign Ro rejoins the *Enterprise*, having been specially trained to seek out and infiltrate a revolutionary group, the Maquis. The Maquis are former Federation colonists, angry at the Federation-Cardassian treaty and trying to restart the war.

Ensign Ro, a Bajoran, seems an obvious choice to infiltrate the terrorists, but she is sorely tempted by their position, and must decide whether to remain loyal to the Federation or to avenge Bajor with the Maquis.

"All Good Things" is the two-hour episode marking the end of seven very successful years on television. The show weaves together the past and future of the *Enterprise*-D, revisiting old scenes from "Farpoint" and other shows and projecting possible futures for the crew members.

Picard has grown into an old man, retired and living in rural France, when Q enters his life once more. Cut loose in time, Picard moves back and forth between three critical time periods, including the "present." A strange and powerful enemy can only be destroyed by three simultaneous attacks, across time, from Picard's *Enterprise*.

As captain of the ship, Picard has little trouble managing events in the past. The real challenge comes when he must return from retirement and, by calling in favors from Captain Beverly Crusher, Admiral Riker, and Professor Data, commandeer the newest *Enterprise* and defeat the enemy. He is successful, and the show miraculously returns to the younger Picard, in his usual place as captain of the *Enterprise*-D.

"All Good Things" ends up being a disappointing finale to *Star Trek: The Next Generation*. The universe seems to be finally coming apart, and with viewers aware that no further episodes are planned, anything could happen. However, in spite of speculation about the future—and the requisite promotions all *Enterprise* officers get before the first movie—in the end the episode returns firmly to the familiar present. For a story where, for a while, anything—including the remaking of the universe—was possible, the return to normalcy is a disappointing denouement. After seven years and 176 episodes, the *Enterprise* in "All Good Things" does not truly go where no one has gone before.

CHAPTER TWELVE:

THE FUTURE BECKONS, BRIGHT AND BOLD

And so *Star Trek,* in its many forms, continues to press on. The original cast and crew have long been enthroned in television and entertainment history. With the finish of *Star Trek: The Next Generation,* yet another *Enterprise* passes into Federation history, leaving the space station *Deep Space Nine* and the wandering starship *Voyager* to continue the exploration of the galaxy. If *Trek* history holds true, these voyages will introduce not only new and wondrous worlds and aliens, but new horizons in man's knowledge of himself and his place in the universe.

As the legacy continues, some of *Star Trek*'s brightest stars are retired, or on leave, from their Starfleet commissions, but continue active entertainment careers. Leonard Nimoy continues to gain fame as a director, has developed a new comic book series called *Primortals,* and is contemplating a sequel to his book, *I Am Not Spock.*

William Shatner, the author of several autobiographical books, also writes *Star Trek* novels for an appreciative audience. The next generation is just getting accustomed to "life after *Trek*." Patrick Stewart has lined up movie roles that take him far from Federation space. Jonathan Frakes has already turned up on *Deep Space Nine* and, as Admiral Riker from "All Good Things," on a Caribbean postage stamp. A team to the end, crewmembers Brent Spiner, Jonathan Frakes, LeVar Burton, Michael Dorn, and Patrick Stewart may sing their way to fame as "The Sun Spots," whose first CD was released this spring. All former cast members continue to explore strange new worlds.

Star Trek's future is by no means limited to the two current television series. As always, *Trek* fans are active at conventions, discussions, parties and gatherings both official and impromptu. The information superhighway abounds with Trekkers using cyberspace to communicate their ideas about, and love for, Gene Roddenberry's brightly imagined worlds. *Star Trek* novels sell millions of copies to hungry fans, giving many readers their first taste of the science fiction novel. And never forget the merchandise, authorized and bootleg, that allows fans to dress like Data, shoot a phaser like Spock, or play an interactive board game about the Klingon Civil War.

The future of *Star Trek,* like its historic popularity, does not rest simply on the entertainment value of the first shows and their successors. From the very beginning, Gene Roddenberry used the voyages of the starship *Enterprise* to explore many kinds of space, peopled by aliens both strange and horrifyingly familiar. The anti-Vietnam sentiment of "A Private Little War" gave way to the cold-war politics exemplified in *The Next Generation*'s inviolable Neutral Zone, demonstrating the shift in American politics from combat to detante. *Deep*

Space Nine explores the growing pains of Bajor, a beleaguered planet just liberated, like much of Eastern Europe, from a long hostile occupation.

Through all four series run classic themes of internal and personal conflict, beginning with Spock's reluctant humanity, to Data's fight with his brother Lore, Commander Sisko's troubles raising his son alone, and the holographic Dr. Zimmerman's struggle to earn a place in the crew of *Voyager*. If *Star Trek*'s settings are wildly different from the lives of its viewers, the passions and dreams of the characters are not.

Current, critical, sharply insightful, often humorous, *Star Trek, The Next Generation, Deep Space Nine, Voyager* and all seven movies never fail to excite, enthrall, and entertain. When all is said and done, the political and psychological commentary discarded, one thing remains: *Star Trek* is enormous fun, and likely to stay that way.

Producers Rick Berman, Michael Piller, and Jeri Taylor are publicly cautious about the future of their *Trek* projects. In a spring 1995 collector's edition of *TV Guide,* Jeri Taylor described one of her most pressing concerns about *Voyager,* "That we don't get comfortable. We are always very mindful that there could be a backlash. Assuming that the audience loves us no matter what—that they'll hang with *Voyager* for seven years and then want to see us on the big screen like *The Next Generation*—is a very dangerous state of mind in which to work. A little bit of fear keeps you juiced."

But *Star Trek,* like the *Enterprise* itself, thrives on uncertainty and adversity, and if the show's producers take a diplomatically cautious line, its captains remain true to form, gambling on present and future in classic adventure style. James T. Kirk, like Gene Roddenberry himself, was a valiant optimist in the face of the worst possible odds, and that spirit has never been lost. As

William Shatner so succinctly put it in his book *Star Trek Memories* (1994), "Nothing is more certain than the fact that *Star Trek*'s wondrous mission has just begun."

CHAPTER THIRTEEN:

CHECKLISTS

LASSIC *STAR TREK*

Episodes are listed in the order in which they first aired on television

FIRST SEASON (1966-67)

PILOT "The Cage"; written by Gene Roddenberry; directed by Robert Butler. Never aired in original form.

1. "The Man Trap"; written by George Clayton Johnson; directed by Marc Daniels
   Guest Cast: Jeanne Bal, Alfred Ryder

2. "Charlie X"; play by D. C. Fontana; Gene Roddenberry; directed by Lawrence Dobkin
   Guest Cast: Robert Walker

3. "Where No Man Has Gone Before"; written by Samuel A. Peeples; directed by James Goldstone

Guest Cast: Gary Lockwood, Sally Kellerman,
Paul Carr, Lloyd Haynes   .

4. "The Naked Time"; written by John D. F. Black;
directed by Marc Daniels
Guest Cast: Bruce Hyde, Stewart Moss

5. "The Enemy Within"; written by Richard Matheson;
directed by Leo Penn
Guest Cast: Jim Goodwin, Edward Madden,
Garland Thompson

6. "Mudd's Women"; directed by Harvey Hart
Guest Cast: Roger C. Carmel, Karen Steele,
Susan Denberg, Maggie Thrett, Gene Dynarski,
Jim Goodwin

7. "What Are Little Girls Made Of?"; written by
Robert Bloch; directed by James Goldstone
Guest Cast: Michael Strong, Sherry Jackson,
Ted Cassidy

8. "Miri"; written by Adrian Spies; directed by
Vincent McEveety
Guest Cast: Kim Darby, Michael J. Pollard,
Jim Goodwin, John Megna, Ed McCready

9. "Dagger of the Mind"; written by S. Bar David;
directed by Vincent McEveety
Guest Cast: James Gregory, Morgan Woodward,
Marianna Hill, Suzanne Wasson

10. "The Corbomite Maneuver"; written by Jerry Sohl;
directed by Joseph Sargent
Guest Cast: Anthony Call, Clint Howard

11. "The Menagerie, Part I"; written by Gene
Roddenberry; directed by Marc Daniels
Guest Cast: Sean Kenney, Malachi Throne,
Julie Parrish, Jeffrey Hunter, John Hoyt, Susan
Oliver, Majel Barrett, Laurel Goodwin, Peter
Duryea, Meg Wyllie, Jon Lormer

12. "The Menagerie, Part II"; written by Gene
Roddenberry; directed by Robert Butler

13. "The Conscience of the King"; written by
    Barry Trivers; directed by Gerd Oswald
    Guest Cast: Arnold Moss, Barbara Anderson,
    Bruce Hyde, Eddie Paskey, William Sargent
14. "Balance of Terror"; written by Paul Schneider;
    directed by Vincent McEveety
    Guest Cast: Mark Lenard, Paul Comi,
    Lawrence Montaigne, John Warburton,
    Stephen Mines, Barbara Baldavin
15. "Shore Leave"; written by Theodore Sturgeon;
    directed by Robert Sparr
    Guest Cast: Barbara Baldavin, Oliver McGowan,
    Perry Lopez, Bruce Mars, Shirley Bonne
16. "The Galileo Seven"; written by Oliver Crawford
    and S. Bar David; directed by Robert Gist
    Guest Cast: Don Marchall, Peter Marko,
    Reese Vaughn, Grant Woods, Phyllis Douglas,
    John Crawford
17. "The Squire of Gothos"; written by Paul Schneider;
    directed by Don McDougall
    Guest Cast: William Campbell, Richard Carlyle,
    Michael Barrier, Venita Wolf
18. "Arena"; written by Gene L. Coon, from the story
    by Fredric L. Brown; directed by Joseph Pevney
    Guest Cast: Carole Shelyne, Jerry Ayres,
    Grant Woods, Tom Troupe, James Farley,
    Sean Kenney
19. "Tomorrow Is Yesterday"; written by
    D. C. Fontana; directed by Michael O'Herlihy
    Guest Cast: Roger Perry, Sherry Townsend,
    Hal Lynch, Ed Peck, John Winston,
    Mark Dempsey
20. "Court Martial"; written by Don M. Mankiewicz
    and Stephen W. Carabatsos; directed by
    Marc Daniels
    Guest Cast: Percy Rodriguez, Elisha Cook Jr.,

Joan Marshall, Richard Webb, Alice Rawlings,
Hagen Beggs

21. "The Return of the Archons"; written by
Gene Roddenberry and Boris Sobelman;
directed by Joseph Pevney
Guest Cast: Harry Townes, Torin Thatcher,
Charles Macauley, Christopher Held,
Brioni Farrell, Jon Lormer, Morgan Farley,
Sid Haig, Ralph Maurer, Eddie Paskey,
Sean Morgan

22. "Space Seed"; written by Gene L. Coon and
Carey Wilber; directed by Marc Daniels
Guest Cast: Ricardo Montalban, Madlyn Rhue,
Blaisdell MaKee, Mark Tobin, John Winston

23. "A Taste of Armageddon"; written by
Robert Hammer and Gene L. Coon;
directed by Joseph Pevney
Guest Cast: Gene Lyons, David Opatoshu,
Robert Samson, Barbara Babcock, Miko Mayama,
Sean Kenney

24. "This Side of Paradise"; written by Nathan Butler
and D. C. Fontana; directed by Ralph Senensky
Guest Cast: Eddie Paskey, Jill Ireland,
Frank Overton, Grant Woods

25. "The Devil in the Dark"; written by Gene L. Coon;
directed by Joseph Pevney
Guest Cast: Ken Lynch, Barry Russo,
Brad Weston, John Cavett, Janos Prohaska,
Biff Elliot, Dick Dial

26. "Errand of Mercy"; written by Gene L. Coon;
directed by John Newland
Guest Cast: David Hillary Hughes, Jon Abbott,
John Colicos, Peter Brocco, Victor Lundin,
George Sawaya, Walt Davis

27. "The Alternative Factor"; written by Don Ingalls;
directed by Gerd Oswald

Guest Cast: Robert Brown, Janet MacLachlen,
Richard Derr, Eddie Paskey

28. "The City on the Edge of Forever"; written by
Harlan Ellison; directed by Joseph Pevney
Guest Cast: Joan Collins, David L. Ross,
Hal Boylor, John Harmon, John Winston

29. "Operation: Annihilate!"; written by Stephen W.
Carabatsos; directed by Herschel Daugherty
Guest Cast: Dave Armstrong, Craig Hundley,
Joan Swift, Maurishka Talifero

SECOND SEASON (1967-68)

30. "Amok Time"; written by Theodore Sturgeon;
directed by Joseph Pevney
Guest Cast: Arlene Martel, Celia Lovsky,
Lawrence Montaigne, Byron Morrow

31. "Who Mourns for Adonais?"; written by
Gilbert Ralston; directed by Marc Daniels
Guest Cast: Michael Forest, Leslie Parrish,
John Winston

32. "The Changeling"; written by John Meredyth Lucas;
directed by Marc Daniels
Guest Cast: Blaisdell Makee, Barbara Gates,
Arnold Lessing, Vic Perrin

33. "Mirror, Mirror"; written by Jerome Bixby;
directed by Joseph Pevney
Guest Cast: Barbara Luna, Vic Perrin, Pete Kellett,
Garth Pillsbury, John Winston

34. "The Apple"; written by Max Ehrlich; directed by
Joseph Pevney
Guest Cast: John Winston, Keith Andes,
Celeste Yarnall, Shari Nims, David Soul,
Mal Friedman, Jerry Daniels, Jay Jones,
Dick Dial

35. "The Doomsday Machine"; written by
Norman Spinrad; directed by Marc Daniels

Guest Cast: William Windom, Elizabeth Rogers, John Copage, Richard Compton

36. "Catspaw"; written by Robert Bloch; directed by Joseph Pevney
Guest Cast: Michael Barrier, Antoinette Bower, Theo Marcuse, Jimmy Jones

37. "I, Mudd"; written by Stephen Kandel; directed by Marc Daniels
Guest Cast: Roger C. Carmel, Kay Elliot, Richard Tatro, Rhae and Alyce Andrece, Tom and Ted LeGarde, Maureen and Colleen Thornton, Tamara and Starr Wilson, Mike Howden, Michael Zaslow

38. "Metamorphosis"; written by Gene L. Coon; directed by Ralph Senesky
Guest Cast: Elinor Donahue, Glenn Corbett

39. "Journey to Babel"; written by D. C. Fontana; directed by Joseph Pevney
Guest Cast: Mark Lenard, Jane Wyatt, William O'Connell, Reggie Nalder, John Wheeler

40. "Friday's Child"; written by D. C. Fontana; directed by Joseph Pevney
Guest Cast: Julie Newmar, Tige Andrews, Michael Dante, Cal Bolder, Ben Gage

41. "The Deadly Years"; written by David P. Harmon; directed by Joseph Pevney
Guest Cast: Charles Drake, Sarah Marshall, Beverly Washburn, Felix Locher, Laura Wood, Carolyn Nelson

42. "Obsession"; written by Art Wallace; directed by Ralph Senensky
Guest Cast: Stephen Brooks, Jerry Ayers

43. "Wolf in the Fold"; written by Robert Bloch; directed by Joseph Pevney
Guest Cast: John Fielder, Charles Macauley, Pilar Seurat, Joseph Bernard, Charles Dierkop,

Judy McConnell, Virginia Aldridge, Judi Sherven, Tania Lemani

44. "The Trouble with Tribbles"; written by David Gerrold; directed by Joseph Pevney
    Guest Cast: William Schallert, William Campbell, Stanley Adams, Whit Bissel, Michael Pataki, Charlie Brill, Ed Reimers, Guy Raymond

45. "The Gamesters of Triskelion"; written by Margaret Armen; directed by Gene Nelson
    Guest Cast: Joseph Ruskin, Angelique Pettyjohn, Steve Sandor, Mickey Morton, Victoria George, Jane Ross, Dick Crocket

46. "A Piece of the Action"; written by David P. Harmon and Gene L. Coon; directed by James Komack
    Guest Cast: William Blackburn, Anthony Caruso, Victor Tayback, Lee Delano, Steve Marlo, John Harmon, Sheldon Collins

47. "The Immunity Syndrome"; written by Robert Sabaroff; directed by Joseph Pevney
    No Guest Cast

48. "A Private Little War"; written by Judd Crucis and Gene Roddenberry; directed by Marc Daniels
    Guest Cast: Michael Whitney, Nancy Kovack, Booker Marshall, Arthur Bernard, Ned Romero, Gary Pillar, Janos Prohaska

49. "Return to Tomorrow"; written by John Kingsbridge; directed by Ralph Senensky
    Guest Cast: Diana Muldaur

50. "Patterns of Force"; written by John Meredyth Lucas; directed by Vincent McEvee
    Guest Cast: David Brian, Skip Homeier, Richard Evans, Valora Norland, William Wintersole, Patrick Horgan, Ralph Maurer, Gilbert Green

51. "By Any Other Name"; written by Jerome Bixby and D. C. Fontana; directed by Marc Daniels

Guest Cast: Warren Stevens, Barbara Bouchet,
Stewart Moss, Robert Fortier, Carol Byrd,
Leslie Dalton, Julie Cobb

52. "Omega Glory"; written by Gene Roddenberry;
directed by Vincent McEveety
Guest Cast: Morgan Woodward, Roy Jensen,
Irene Kelley, David L. Ross, Eddie Paskey,
Ed McCready, Lloyd Kino, Morgan Farley

53. "The Ultimate Computer"; written by Lawrence
Wolfe and D. C. Fontana; directed by
John Meredyth Lucas
Guest Cast: William Marshall, Barry Russo,
Sean Morgan

54. "Bread and Circuses"; Gene Roddenberry and
Gene L. Coon, directed by Ralph Senensky
Guest Cast: William Smithers, Logan Ramsey,
Ian Wolfe, Rhodes Reason, Lois Jewell

55. "Assignment: Earth"; written by Art Wallace and
Gene Roddenberry; directed by Marc Daniels
Guest Cast: Robert Lansing, Teri Garr,
Don Keefer, Morgan Jones, Lincoln Demyan

THIRD SEASON (1968-69)

56. "Spock's Brain"; written by Lee Cronin;
(pseudonym for Gene L. Coon); directed by
Marc Daniels
Guest Cast: Marj Dusay, James Daris,
Sheila Leighton

57. "The *Enterprise* Incident"; written by D. C. Fontana;
directed by John Meredyth Lucas
Guest Cast: Joanne Linville, Jack Donner,
Richard Compton

58. "The Paradise Syndrome"; written by Margaret
Armen; directed by Jud Taylor
Guest Cast: Sabrina Scharf, Rudy Solari,
Richard Hale, Sean Morgan, Lamont Laird

59. "And the Children Shall Lead"; written by
Edward J. Lakso; directed by Marvin Chomsky
Guest Cast: Melvin Belli, Craig Hundley,
James Wellman, Pamelyn Ferdin, Brian Tochi,
Caesar Belli, Mark Robert Brown

60. "Is There in Truth No Beauty?"; written by
Jean Lisette Aroeste; directed by Ralph Senensky
Guest Cast: Diana Muldaur, David Frankham

61. "Spectre of the Gun"; written by Lee Cronin;
directed by Vincent McEveety
Guest Cast: Bonnie Beecher, Rex Holman,
Ron Soble, Charles Maxwell, Sam Gilman,
Bill Zuckert, Charles Seel, Ed McReady,
Gregg Palmer

62. "Day of the Dove"; written by Jerome Bixby;
directed by Marvin Chomsky
Guest Cast: Michael Ansara, Susan Johnson,
David L. Rose, Mark Tobin

63. "For the World Is Hollow and I Have Touched the
Sky"; written by Rick Vollaerts; directed by
Tony Leader
Guest Cast: Kate Woodville, Byron Morrow,
Jon Lormer

64. "The Tholian Web"; written by Judy Burns and
Chet Richards; directed by Herb Wallerstein
Guest Cast: Voice of Barbara Babcock

65. "Plato's Stepchildren"; written by Meyer Dolinsky;
directed by David Alexander
Guest Cast: Michael Dunn, Liam Sullivan,
Barbara Babcock, Tedd Scott, Derek Partridge

66. "Wink of an Eye"; written by Arthur Heineman and
Lee Cronin; directed by Jud Taylor
Guest Cast: Kathie Brown, Geoffrey Binney,
Eric Holland, Jason Evers

67. "The Empath"; written by Joyce Muskat; directed by
John Erman

Guest Cast: Kathryn Hays, Willard Sage,
Alan Bergman, David Roberts, Jason Wingreen
68. "Elaan of Troyius"; written and directed by
John Meredyth Lucas
Guest Cast: France Nuyen, Jay Robinson,
Tony Young, Victor Brandt, K. L. Smith,
Lee Duncan
69. "Whom Gods Destroy"; written by Lee Erwin and
Jerry Sohl; directed by Herb Wallerstein
Guest Cast: Steve Inhat, Yvonne Craig,
Keye Luke, Richard Geary, Tony Downey
70. "Let That Be Your Last Battlefield"; written by
Lee Cronin and Oliver Crawford; directed by
Jud Taylor
Guest Cast: Lou Antonio, Frank Gorshin
71. "The Mark of Gideon"; written by George F. Slavin
and Stanley Adams; directed by Jud Taylor
Guest Cast: Sharon Acker, David Hurst,
Gene Dynarsky, Richard Derr
72. "That Which Survives"; written by D. C. Fontana
and George Meredyth Lucas; directed by
Michael Richards
Guest Cast: Lee Meriwether, Naomi Pollack,
Arthur Batanides, Brad Forrest, Kenneth
Washington, Booker Marshall
73. "The Lights of Zetar"; written by Shari Lewis and
Jeremy Tarcher; directed by Herb Kenwith
Guest Cast: Jan Shutan, John Winston,
Libby Erwin
74. "Requiem for Methuselah"; written by Jerome Bixby;
directed by Murray Golden
Guest Cast: James Daly, Louise Sorel,
John Buonomo
75. "The Way to Eden"; written by Michael Richards
and Arthur Heinemann; directed by David
Guest Cast: Skip Homeier, Mary Linda Rapelye,

Victor Brandt, Charles Napler, Deborah Downey,
Phyllis Douglas, Elizabeth Rogers

76. "The Cloud Minders"; written by Oliver Crawford,
Margaret Armen, and David Gerrold; directed by
Jud Taylor
Guest Cast: Jeff Corey, Diana Ewing,
Charlene Polite, Fred Williamson, Ed Long

77. "The Savage Curtain"; written by Gene Roddenberry
and Arthur Heinemann; directed by
Herschel Daugherty
Guest Cast: Phillip Pine, Carol Daniels Dement,
Lee Bergere, Barry Atwater, Nathan Jung,
Robert Herron, Avell Blanton

78. "All Our Yesterdays"; written by Jean Lisette
Aroeste; directed by Marvin Chomsky
Guest Cast: Mariette Hartley, Ian Wolfe,
Anna Karen, Johnny Haymer, Ed Bakey,
Kermit Murdock, Al Cavens, Stan Barrett

79. "Turnabout Intruder"; written by Gene Roddenberry
and Arthur H. Singer; directed by Herb Wallerstein
Guest Cast: Sandra Smith, Harry Landers,
Barbara Baldavin, Roger Halloway

ANIMATED STAR TREK

1. "Beyond the Farthest Star"; written by
   Samuel A. Peeples
2. "Yesteryear"; written by D. C. Fontana
3. "One of Our Planets Is Missing"; written by
   Marc Daniels
4. "The Lorelei Signal"; written by Margaret Armen
5. "More Tribbles, More Troubles"; written by
   David Gerrold
6. "The Survivor"; written by James Schmerer
7. "The Infinite Vulcan"; written by Walter Koenig
8. "The Magicks of Megas-Tu"; written by
   Larry Brody
9. "Once Upon a Planet"; written by Chuck Menville
   and Len Jenson
10. "Mudd's Passion"; written by Stephen Kandel

11. "The Terratin Incident"; written by Paul Schneider
12. "The Time Trap"; written by Joyce Perry
13. "The Ambergris Element"; written by Margaret Armen
14. "The Slaver Weapon"; written by Larry Niven (from his story "The Soft Weapon")
15. "The Eye of the Beholder"; written by David P. Harmon
16. "The Jihad"; written by Stephen J. Kandel
17. "The Pirates of Orion"; written by Howard Weinstein
18. "Bem"; written by David Gerrold
19. "The Practical Joker"; written by Chuck Menville
20. "Albatross"; written by Dario Finelli
21. "How Sharper Than a Serpent's Tooth"; written by Russell Bates and David Wise
22. "The Counter-Clock Incident"; written by John Culver

HE NEXT GENERATION

SEASON ONE (1987-88)

1 & 2. "Encounter at Farpoint" (Two hours)
Written by D. C. Fontana and Gene Roddenberry;
Directed by Corey Allen
Guest Cast: John deLancie, Michael Bell,
DeForest Kelley, Colm Meaney, Cary Hiroyuki,
Timothy Dang, David Erskine, Evelyn Guerrero,
Chuck Hicks

3. "The Naked Now"
Teleplay by J. Michael Bingham; Story by
John D. F. Black and J. Michael Bingham; Directed
by Paul Lynch
Guest Cast: Benjamin W. S. Lum, Michael Rider,
David Renan, Skip Stellrecht, Kenny Koch

4. "Code of Honor"
   Teleplay by Kathryn Powers and Michael Baron;
   Directed by Russ Mayberry
   Guest Cast: Jessie Lawrence Ferguson,
   Karole Selmon, James Louis Watkins,
   Michael Rider

5. "The Last Outpost"
   Teleplay by Herbert Wright; Story by
   Richard Krzemian; Directed by Richard Colla
   Guest Cast: Darryl Henriques, Mike Gomez,
   Armin Shimerman, Jake Dengal, Tracey Walter

6. "Where No One Has Gone Before"
   Written by Diane Duane and Michael Reaves;
   Directed by Rob Bowman
   Guest Cast: Biff Yeager, Charles Dayton,
   Victoria Dillard, Stanley Kamel, Eric Menyuk,
   Herta Ware

7. "Lonely Among Us"
   Script by D. C. Fontana; Story by Michael Halperin;
   Directed by Cliff Bole
   Guest Cast: Colm Meaney, Kavi Raz, John Durbin

8. "Justice"
   Teleplay by Worley Thorne; Story by
   Ralph Willis and Worley Thorne; Directed by
   James L. Conway
   Guest Cast: Josh Clark; David Q. Combs;
   Richard Lavin; Judith Jones; Eric Matthew;
   Brad Zerbst; David Michael Graves

9. "The Battle"
   Teleplay by Herbert Wright; Story by
   Larry Forester; Directed by Rob Bowman
   Guest Cast: Frank Corsentino, Doug Warhit,
   Robert Towers

10. "Hide and Q"
    Teleplay by C. J. Holland and Gene Roddenberry;
    Story by C. J. Holland; Directed by Cliff Bole

Guest Cast: John deLancie, Elaine Nalee,
William A. Wallace

11. "Haven"
Teleplay by Tracy Tormé; Story by Tracy Tormé
and Lian Okun; Directed by Richard Compton
Guest Cast: Danzita Kingsley, Carel Struycken,
Anna Katrina, Raye Birk, Michael Rider,
Majel Barrett, Rob Knepper, Nan Martin,
Robert Ellenstein

12. "The Big Goodbye"
Written by Tracy Tormé; Directed by
Joseph L. Scanlan
Guest Cast: Mike Genovese, Dick Miller,
Carolyn Alport, Rhonda Aldrich, Eric Cord,
Lawrence Tierney, Harvey Jason, William Boyett,
David Selburg, Gary Armagnal

13. "Datalore"
Teleplay by Robert Lewin and Gene Roddenberry;
Story by Robert Lewin and Maurice Hurley;
Directed by Rob Bowman
Guest Cast: Biff Yeager

14. "Angel One"
Teleplay by Patrick Berry; Directed by Michael
Rhodes
Guest Cast: Karen Montgomery, Sam Hennings,
Leonard John Crowfoot, Patricia McPherson

15. "11001001"
Written by Maurice Hurley and Robert Lewin;
Directed by Paul Lynch
Guest Cast: Carolyn McCormick, Iva Lane;
Kelly Ann McNally, Jack Sheldon,
Abdul Salaam El Razzac, Ron Brown,
Gene Dynarski, Katy Boyer, Alexandra Johnson

16. "Too Short a Season"
Teleplay by Michael Michaelian and D. C. Fontana;
Story by Michael Michaelian; Directed by

Rob Bowman
Guest Cast: Clayton Rohner, Marsha Hunt,
Michael Pataki

17. "When the Bough Breaks"
Teleplay by Hannah Louise Shearer; Directed by
Kim Manners
Guest Cast: Dierk Torsek, Michele Marsh,
Dan Mason, Philip N. Waller, Connie Danese,
Jessica and Vanessa Bova, Jerry Hardin, Brenda
Strong, Jandi Swanson, Paul Lambert, Ivy Bethune

18. "Home Soil"
Teleplay by Robert Sabaroff; Story by Karl Guers,
Ralph Sanchez, and Robert Sabaroff; Directed by
Corey Allen
Guest Cast: Walter Gotell, Elizabeth Lidsey,
Mario Roccuzzo, Carolyn Barry, Gerard Pendergast

19. "Coming of Age"
Written by Sandy Fries; Directed by Michael Vejar
Guest Cast: Estée Chandler; Daniel Riordan,
Brendan McKane, Wyatt Knight, Ward Costello,
Robert Schenkkan, Robert Ito, John Putch,
Stephan Gregory, Tasia Valenza

20. "Heart of Glory"
Teleplay by Maurice Hurley; Story by Maurice
Hurley, Herb Wright, and D. C. Fontana; Directed
by Rob Bowman
Guest Cast: Vaughn Armstrong, Robert Bauer,
Brad Zerbst, Dennis Madalone, Charles H. Hyman

21. "Arsenal of Freedom"
Teleplay by Richard Manning and Hans Beimler;
Story by Maurice Hurley and Robert Lewin;
Directed by Les Landau
Guest Cast: Vincent Schiavelli, Marco Rodriguez,
Vyto Ruginis, Julia Nickson, George De La Pena

22. "Symbiosis"
Teleplay by Robert Lewin, Richard Manning, and

Hans Beimler; Story by Robert Lewin; Directed by
Win Phelps
Guest Cast: Merritt Butrick, Judson Scott,
Kimberly Farr, Richard Lineback

23. "Skin of Evil"
Teleplay by Joseph Stefano and Hannah Louise
Shearer; Story by Joseph Stefano; Directed by
Joseph L. Scanlan
Guest Cast: Ron Gans as the voice of Armus,
Walker Boone, Brad Zerbst, Raymond Forchion,
Mart McChesney

24. "We'll Always Have Paris"
Teleplay by Deborah Dean Davis and Hannah
Louise Shearer; Directed by Robert Becker
Guest Cast: Isabel Lorca, Rod Loomis, Dan Kern,
Jean-Paul Vignon, Kelly Ashmore,
Lance Spellerberg, Michelle Phillips

25. "Conspiracy"
Teleplay by Tracy Tormé; Story by Robert Sabaroff;
Directed by Cliff Bole;
Guest Cast: Michael Berryman, Ursaline Bryant,
Henry Darrow, Robert Schenkkan,
Jonathan Farwell

26. "The Neutral Zone"
Television story and teleplay by Maurice Hurley;
Story by Deborah McIntyre and Mona Clee;
Directed by James L. Conway
Guest Cast: Marc Alaimo, Anthony James,
Leon Rippy, Gracie Harrison

SEASON TWO (1988-89)

27. "The Child"
Written by Jaron Summer, Jon Povil, and Maurice
Hurley; Directed by Rob Bowman
Guest Cast: Whoopi Goldberg, Seymour Cassel,
R. J. Williams, Dawn Arnemann, Zachary

Benjamin, Dore Keller

28. "Where Silence Has Lease"
Written by Jack B. Sowards; Directed by
Winrich Kolbe
Guest Cast: Colm Meaney, Earl Boen,
Charles Douglass

29. "Elementary, Dear Data"
Written by Brian Alan Lane; Directed by
Rob Bowman
Guest Cast: Daniel Davis, Alan Shearman,
Biff Manard, Diz White, Anne Ramsey,
Richard Merson

30. "The Outrageous Okona"
Teleplay by Burton Armus; Story by Les Menchen,
Lance Dickson, David Lansburg, and Burton Armus,
Directed by Robert Becker
Guest Cast: Joe Piscopo, William O. Campbell,
Douglas Rowe, Albert Stratton; Kieran Mulroney

31. "The Schizoid Man"
Teleplay by Tracy Tormé; Story by Richard
Manning and Hans Beimler; Directed by
Les Landau
Guest Cast: W. Morgan Sheppard, Suzie Plakson,
Barbara Alyn Woods

32. "Loud as a Whisper"
Written by Jacqueline Zambrano; Directed by
Larry Shaw
Guest Cast: Howie Seago, Marnie Mosiman,
Thomas Oglesby, Leo Damian

33. "Unnatural Selection"
Written by John Mason and Mike Gray; Directed by
Paul Lynch
Guest Cast: Colm Meaney, Patricia Smith,
J. Patrick McNamara, Scott Trost, George Baxter

34. "A Matter of Honor"
Teleplay by Burton Armus; Story by

Wanda M. Haight, Gregory Amos, and Burton
Armus; Directed by Rob Bowman
Guest Cast: John Putch, Christopher Collins,
Brian Thompson, Laura Drake, Peter Parros

35. "The Measure of a Man"
Written by Melinda M. Snodgrass; Directed by
Robert Scheerer
Guest Cast: Whoopi Goldberg, Colm Meaney,
Amanda McBroom, Clyde Kusatsu, Brian Brophy

36. "The Dauphin"
Written by Scott Rubinstein and Leonard Mlodinow;
Directed by Rob Bowman
Guest Cast: Paddi Edwards, Jamie Hubbard,
Mädchen Amick, Cindy Sorenson, Jennifer Barlow,
Peter Neptune

37. "Contagion"
Written by Steve Gerber and Beth Woods; Directed
by Joseph L. Scanlan
Guest Cast: Colm Meaney, Thalmus Rasulala,
Carolyn Seymour, Dana Sparks, Folkert Schmidt

38. "The Royale"
Written by Keith Mills; Directed by Cliff Bole
Guest Cast: Colm Meaney, Sam Anderson,
Jill Jacobson, Leo Garcia, Gregory Beecroft

39. "Time Squared"
Teleplay by Maurice Hurley; Story by Kurt Michael
Bensmiller; Directed by Joseph L. Scanlan
Guest Cast: Colm Meaney

40. "The Icarus Factor"
Teleplay by David Assael and Robert L.
McCullough; Story by David Assael; Directed by
Robert Iscove
Guest Cast: Colm Meaney, Mitchell Ryan,
Lance Spellerberg

41. "Pen Pals"
Teleplay by Melinda M. Snodgrass; Story by

Hannah Louise Shearer; Directed by Winrich Kolbe
Guest Cast: Colm Meaney, Nicholas Cascone,
Nikki Cox, Ann H. Gillespie, Whitney Rydbeck

42. "Q Who"
Written by Maurice Hurley; Directed by
Rob Bowman
Guest Cast: Whoopi Goldberg, Colm Meaney,
John deLancie, Lycia Naff

43. "Samaritan Snare"
Written by Robert L. McCullough; Directed by
Les Landau
Guest Cast: Christopher Collins, Leslie Morris,
Daniel Bemzau, Lycia Naff, Tzi Ma

44. "Up the Long Ladder"
Written by Melinda M. Snodgrass; Directed by
Winrich Kolbe
Guest Cast: Colm Meaney, Barrie Ingham,
Jon de Vries, Rosalyn Landor

45. "Manhunt"
Written by Terry Devereaux; Directed by
Rob Bowman
Guest Cast: Colm Meaney, Majel Barrett,
Robert Costanzo, Rod Arrants, Carel Struycken,
Robert O'Reilly, Rhonda Aldrich, Mick Fleetwood,
Wren T. Brown

46. "The Emissary"
Television story and teleplay by Richard Manning
and Hans Beimler; Story by Thomas H. Calder;
Directed by Cliff Bole
Guest Cast: Colm Meaney, Suzie Plakson, Georgann
Johnson, Anne Elizabeth Ramsey, Dietrich Bader

47. "Peak Performance"
Written by David Kemper; Directed by
Robert Scheerer
Guest Cast: Roy Brocksmith; Armin Shimerman;
David L. Lander, Leslie Neale, Glenn Morshower

48. "Shades of Grey"
    Teleplay by Maurice Hurley, Richard Manning, and
    Hans Beimler; Story by Maurice Hurley; Directed
    by Rob Bowman
    Guest Cast: Colm Meaney

SEASON THREE (1989-90)

49. "Evolution"
    Teleplay by Michael Piller; Story by Michael Piller
    and Michael Wagner; Directed by Winrich Kolbe
    Guest Cast: Whoopi Goldberg, Ken Jenkins,
    Mary McCusker, Randall Patrick, Scott Grimes,
    Amy O'Neill
50. "The Ensigns of Command"
    Written by Melinda M. Snodgrass; Directed by
    Cliff Bole
    Guest Cast: Colm Meaney, Eileen Seeley,
    Mark L. Taylor, Richard Allen, Grainger Hines,
    Mart McChesney
51. "The Survivors"
    Written by Michael Wagner; Directed by
    Les Landau
    Guest Cast: John Anderson, Anne Haney
52. "Who Watches the Watchers"
    Written by Richard Manning and Hans Beimler;
    Directed by Robert Weimer
    Guest Cast: Kathryn Leigh Scott, Ray Wise,
    James Greene, Pamela Segall, John McLiam,
    Lois Hall, James McIntyre
53. "The Bonding"
    Written by Ronald D. Moore; Directed by
    Winrich Kolbe
    Guest Cast: Colm Meaney, Susan Powell,
    Gabriel Damon
54. "Booby Trap"
    Written by Ron Roman, Michael Piller,

Richard Danus, and Michael Wagner; Directed by
Gabrielle Beaumont
Guest Cast: Whoopi Goldberg, Colm Meaney,
Susan Gibney, Albert Hall, Julie Warner

55. "The Enemy"
Written by David Kemper and Michael Piller;
Directed by David Carson
Guest Cast: John Snyder, Andreas Katsulas,
Steven Rankin, Colm Meaney

56. "The Price"
Written by Hannah Louise Shearer; Directed by
Robert Scheerer
Guest Cast: Matt McCoy, Elizabeth Hoffman,
Castulo Guerra, Scott Thomson, Dan Shor,
Kevin Peter Hall, Colm Meaney

57. "The Vengeance Factor"
Written by Sam Rolfe; Directed by Timothy Bond
Guest Cast: Lisa Wilcox, Joey Aresco, Nancy
Parsons, Stephen Lee, Marc Lawrence,
Elkanah J. Burns

58. "The Defector"
Written by Ronald D. Moore; Directed by
Robert Scheerer
Guest Cast: James Sloyan, Andreas Katsulas,
John Hancock, S. A. Templeman

59. "The Hunted"
Written by Robin Berheim; Directed by Cliff Bole
Guest Cast: Jeff McCarthy, James Cromwell,
J. Michael Flynn, Andrew Bicknell, Colm Meaney

60. "The High Ground"
Written by Melinda M. Snodgrass; Directed by
Gabrielle Beaumont
Guest Cast: Kerrie Keene, Richard Cox,
Marc Buckland, Fred G. Smith, Christopher Pettiet

61. "Déjà Q"
Written by Richard Danus; Directed by Les Landau

Guest Cast: Whoopi Goldberg, John deLancie,
Corbin Bernsen, Richard Cansino

62. "A Matter of Perspective"
Written by Ed Zuckerman; Directed by Cliff Bole
Guest Cast: Colm Meaney, Craig Richard Nelson,
Gina Hecht, Mark Margolis, Juli Donald

63. "Yesterday's Enterprise"
Teleplay by Ira Steven Behr, Richard Manning,
Hans Beimler and Ronald D. Moore; Story by
Trent Christopher Ganing and Eric A. Stillwell;
Directed by David Carson
Guest Cast: Whoopi Goldberg, Denise Crosby,
Christopher McDonald, Tricia O'Neil

64. "The Offspring"
Written by René Echeverria; Directed by
Jonathan Frakes
Guest Cast: Hallie Todd, Nicolas Coster,
Judyann Elder, Leonard John Crowfoot,
Diane Moser, Hayne Bayle, Maria Leone,
James G. Becker

65. "Sins of the Father"
Teleplay by Ronald D. Moore and W. Reed Moran;
Story by Drew Deighan; Directed by Les Landau
Guest Cast: Charles Cooper, Tony Todd,
Patrick Massett, Thelma Lee, Teddy Davis

66. "Allegiance"
Written by Richard Manning and Hans Beimler;
Directed by Winrich Kolbe
Guest Cast: Stephen Markle, Reiner Schone,
Joycelyn O'Brien, Jerry Rector, Jeff Rector

67. "Captain's Holiday"
Written by Ira Steven Behr; Directed by
Chip Chalmers
Guest Cast: Jennifer Hetrick, Karen Landry,
Michael Champion, Max Grodenchik,
Deirdre Impershein

68. "Tin Man"
Written by Dennis Putman Bailey and
David Bischoff; Directed by Robert Scheerer
Guest Cast: Harry Groener, Michael Cavanaugh,
Peter Vogt, Colm Meaney

69. "Hollow Pursuits"
Written by Sally Caves; Directed by Cliff Bole
Guest Cast: Dwight Schultz, Charley Lang,
Whoopi Goldberg, Colm Meaney

70. "The Most Toys"
Written by Shari Goodhartz; Directed by
Timothy Bond
Guest Cast: Colm Meaney, Jane Daly,
Nehemiah Persoff, Saul Rubinek

71. "Sarek"
Television story and teleplay by Peter S. Beagle;
Story by Mark Cushman and Jake Jacobs; Directed
by Les Landau
Guest Cast: Mark Lenard, Joanna Miles,
William Denis, Rocco Sisto, John H. Francis,
Colm Meaney

72. "Ménage à Troi"
Written by Fred Bronson and Susan Sackett;
Directed by Robert Legato
Guest Cast: Majel Barrett, Frank Cosentino,
Ethan Phillips, Peter Slutsker, Rudolph Willrich,
Carel Struycken

73. "Transfigurations"
Written by René Echevarria; Directed by
Tom Benko
Guest Cast: Mark La Mura, Charles Dennis,
Julie Warner, Patti Tippo, Colm Meaney

74. "The Best of Both Worlds, Part I"
Written by Michael Piller; Directed by Cliff Bole
Guest Cast: Elizabeth Dennehy, George Murdock,
Whoopi Goldberg

SEASON FOUR (1990-91)

75. "The Best of Both Worlds, Part II"
Written by Michael Piller; Directed by Cliff Bole
Guest Cast: Elizabeth Dennehy, George Murdock,
Whoopi Goldberg, Todd Merrill, Colm Meaney

76. "Family"
Written by Ronald D. Moore; Directed by
Les Landau
Guest Cast: Jeremy Kemp, Samantha Eggar,
Theodore Bikel, Georgia Brown, Dennis Creaghan,
Whoopi Goldberg, Colm Meaney, David Tristan
Birkin, Doug Wert

77. "Brothers"
Written by Rick Berman; Directed by Rob Bowman
Guest Cast: Cory Danzinger, Adam Ryen,
James Lashly, Colm Meaney

78. "Suddenly Human"
Teleplay by John Whelpley and Jeri Taylor; Story
by Ralph Phillips; Directed by Gabrielle Beaumont
Guest Cast: Sherman Howard, Chad Allen,
Barbara Townsend, Sherman Howard

79. "Remember Me"
Written by Lee Sheldon; Directed by Cliff Bole
Guest Cast: Eric Menyuk, Bill Erwin, Colm Meaney

80. "Legacy"
Written by Joe Menosky; Directed by
Robert Scheerer
Guest Cast: Beth Toussaint, Don Mirrault,
Colm Meaney, Vladimir Velasco,
Christopher Michael

81. "Reunion"
Teleplay by Thomas Perry, Jo Perry,
Ronald D. Moore, and Brannon Braga; Story by
Drew Deighan, Thomas Perry, and Jo Perry;
Directed by Jonathan Frakes

Guest Cast: Suzie Plakson, Robert O'Reilly,
Patrick Massett, John Stever, Michael Ridder,
April Grace, Basil Wallace, Mirron E. Willis

82. "Future Imperfect"
Written by J. Larry Carroll and David Bennett
Carren; Directed by Les Landau
Guest Cast: Andreas Katsulas, Chris Demetral,
Carolyn McCormick, April Grace, Patti Yasutake,
Todd Merrill, George O. Hanlon, Jr.

83. "Final Mission"
Teleplay by Kacey Arnold-Ince and Jeri Taylor;
Story by Kacey Arnold-Ince; Directed by
Corey Allen
Guest Cast: Nick Tate, Kim Hamilton, Mary Kohnert

84. "The Loss"
Teleplay by Hilary J. Bader, Alan J. Adler, and
Vanessa Greene; Story by Hilary J. Bader; Directed
by Chip Chalmers
Guest Cast: Kim Braden, Mary Kohnert,
Whoopi Goldberg

85. "Data's Day"
Teleplay by Harold Apter and Ronald D. Moore;
Story by Harold Apter; Directed by Robert Wiemer
Guest Cast: Rosalind Chao, Sierra Pecheur,
Alan Scharfe, Colm Meaney, April Grace, U'Sal

86. "The Wounded"
Teleplay by Jeri Taylor; Story by Stuart Charno,
Sara Charno, and Cy Chermax; Directed by
Chip Chalmers
Guest Cast: Bob Gunton, Rosalind Chao,
Marc Alaimo, Marco Rodriguez, Time Winters,
John Hancock

87. "Devil's Due"
Teleplay by Philip Lazebnik; Story by Philip
Lazebnik and William Douglas Lansford; Directed
by Tom Benko

Guest Cast: Marta DuBois, Paul Lambert, Marcelo Tubert, William Glover, Thad Lamey, Tom Magee

88. "Clues"
Teleplay by Bruce D. Arthurs and Joe Menosky; Story by Bruce D. Arthurs; Directed by Les Landau
Guest Cast: Pamela Winslow, Rhonda Aldrich, Whoopi Goldberg, Colm Meaney, Thomas Knickerbocker

89. "First Contact"
Teleplay by Dennis Russell Bailey, David Bischoff, Joe Menosky, Ronald D. Moore, and Michael Piller; Story by Marc Scott Zicree; Directed by Cliff Bole
Guest Cast: George Coe, Carolyn Seymour, George Hearn, Michael Ensign, Steven Anderson, Sachi Parker, Bebe Neuwirth

90. "Galaxy's Child"
Teleplay by Maurice Hurley; Story by Thomas Kartozian; Directed by Winrich Kolbe
Guest Cast: Susan Gibney, Lanei Chapman, Jana Marie Hupp, Whoopi Goldberg, April Grace

91. "Night Terrors"
Teleplay by Pamela Douglas and Jeri Taylor; Story by Shari Goodhartz; Directed by Les Landau
Guest Cast: Rosalind Chao, John Vickery, Duke Moosekian, Craig Hurley, Brian Tochi, Lanei Chapman, Deborah Taylor, Colm Meaney

92. "Identity Crisis"
Teleplay by Brannon Braga; Story by Timothy DeHaas; Directed by Winrich Kolbe
Guest Cast: Maryann Plunkett, Patti Yasutake, Amick Byram, Dennis Madalone, Mona Grudt, Paul Tompkins

93. "The Nth Degree"
Written by Joe Menosky; Directed by Robert Legato

Guest Cast: Dwight Schultz, Jim Norton,
Saxon Trainor, Page Leong, David Coburn

94. "QPid"
Teleplay by Ira Steven Behr; Story by
Randee Russell and Ira Steven Behr; Directed by
Cliff Bole
Guest Cast: John deLancie, Jennifer Hetrick,
Clive Revill, Joi Staton

95. "The Drumhead"
Written by Jeri Taylor; Directed by Jonathan Frakes
Guest Cast: Jean Simmons, Bruce French,
Spencer Garrett, Henry Woronicz, Earl Billings,
Ann Shea

96. "Half a Life"
Teleplay by Peter Allen Fields; Story by
Ted Roberts and Peter Allen Fields; Directed by
Les Landau
Guest Cast: David Ogden Stiers, Majel Barrett,
Michelle Forbes, Terrence McNally,
Carel Struycken

97. "The Host"
Written by Michel Horvat; Directed by
Marvin V. Rush
Guest Cast: Franc Luz; Barbara Tarbuck,
Nicole Orth-Pallavicini, William Newman,
Patti Yasutake, Robert Harper

98. "The Mind's Eye"
Written by René Echeverria and Ken Schafer;
Directed by David Livingston
Guest Cast: Larry Dobkin, John Fleck,
Denise Crosby, Edward Wiley, Colm Meaney

99. "In Theory"
Written by Joe Menosky and Ronald D. Moore;
Directed by Patrick Stewart
Guest Cast: Whoopi Goldberg, Michele Scarabelli,
Pamela Winslow, Colm Meaney

100. "Redemption, Part I"
Written by Ronald D. Moore; Directed by Cliff Bole
Guest Cast: Whoopi Goldberg, Denise Crosby,
Robert O'Reilly, Tony Todd, Barbara March,
Gwynyth Walsh, Ben Slack, Nicholas Kepros,
J. D. Cullum, Tom Ormeny, Clifton Jones

SEASON FIVE (1991-92)
101. "Redemption, Part II"
Written by Ronald D. Moore; Directed by
D. David Carson
Guest Cast: Denise Crosby, Tony Todd,
Barbara March, Gwynyth Walsh, Jordan Lund,
Stephen James Carver
102. "Darmok"
Teleplay by Joe Menosky and Philip Lazebnik;
Directed by Winrich Kolbe
Guest Cast: Paul Winfield, Richard Allen,
Colm Meaney, Ashley Judd
103. "Ensign Ro"
Teleplay by Michael Piller; Story by Rick Berman
and Michael Piller; Directed by Les Landau
Guest Cast: Michelle Forbes, Scott Marlowe,
Frank Collison, Jeffrey Hayenga, Harley Venton,
Ken Thorley, Cliff Potts
104. "Silicon Avatar"
Teleplay by Jeri Taylor, Story by Lawrence V.
Conley; Directed by Cliff Bole
Guest Cast: Ellen Geer, Susan Diol
105. "Disaster"
Teleplay by Ronald D. Moore; Story by Ron Jarvis
and Philip A. Scorza; Directed by
Gabrielle Beaumont
Guest Cast: Rosalind Chao, Colm Meaney,
Michelle Forbes, Erika Flores, John Christian Grass,
Max Supera, Cameron Arnett, Dana Hupp

106. "The Game"
Teleplay by Brannon Braga; Story by Susan Sackett,
Fred Bronson, and Brannon Braga; Directed by
Corey Allen
Guest Cast: Ashley Judd, Katherine Moffat,
Colm Meaney, Patti Yasutake, Wil Wheaton

107. "Unification, Part I"
Teleplay by Michael Piller; Story by Rick Berman
and Michael Piller; Directed by Cliff Bole
Guest Cast: Joanna Miles, Stephen Root,
William Batiani, Graham Jarvis, Malachi Throne,
Norman Large, Daniel Roebuck, Erick Avari,
Karen Hensel, Mark Lenard, Leonard Nimoy

108. "Unification, Part II"
Teleplay by Michael Piller; Story by Rick Berman
and Michael Piller; Directed by Cliff Bole
Guest Cast: Joanna Miles, Stephen Root,
Graham Jarvis, Malachi Throne, Norman Large,
Daniel Roebuck, Erick Avari, Karen Hensel,
Mark Lenard, Leonard Nimoy, Denise Crosby,
Susan Fallender, Vidal Peterson, Harriet Leider

109. "A Matter of Time"
Written by Rick Berman; Directed by Paul Lynch
Guest Cast: Matt Frewer, Stefan Gierasch,
Sheila Franklin, Shay Garner

110. "New Ground"
Teleplay by Grant Rosenberg; Story by
Sara Charno and Stuart Charno; Directed by
Robert Scheerer
Guest Cast: Brian Bonsall, Georgia Brown,
Jennifer Edwards, Richard McGonagle

111. "Hero Worship"
Teleplay by Joe Menosky; Story by Hilary J. Bader;
Directed by Patrick Stewart
Guest Cast: Joshua Harris, Harley Venton,
Sheila Franklin

112. "Violations"
Teleplay by Pamela Gray and Jeri Taylor; Story by
Shari Goodhartz, T. Michael Gray, and
Pamela Gray; Directed by Robert Wiemer
Guest Cast: David Sage, Eve Brenner,
Rosalind Chao, Ben Lemon, Rick Fitts, Doug Wert,
Craig Benton

113. "Masterpiece Society"
Teleplay by Adam Belanoff and Michael Piller;
Story by James Kahn and Adam Belanoff; Directed
by Winrich Kolbe
Guest Cast: Ron Canada, Dey Young, John Snyder,
Sheila Franklin

114. "Conundrum"
Teleplay by Barry Schkolnick; Story by
Paul Schiffer; Directed by Les Landau
Guest Cast: Erich Anderson, Michelle Forbes,
Liz Vassey, Erick Weiss, Kieran MacDuff

115. "Power Play"
Teleplay by Rene Balcer, Herbert J. Wright and
Brannon Braga; Story by Paul Ruben and Maurice
Hurley; Directed by David Livingston
Guest Cast: Rosalind Chao, Colm Meaney,
Michelle Forbes, Ryan Reid

116. "Ethics"
Teleplay by Ronald D. Moore; Story by Sara Charno
and Stuart Charno; Directed by Chip Chalmers
Guest Cast: Caroline Kava, Brian Bonsall,
Patti Yasutake

117. "The Outcast"
Written by Jeri Taylor; Directed by Robert Scheerer
Guest Cast: Melinda Culea, Callan White,
Megan Cole

118. "Cause and Effect"
Written by Brannon Braga; Directed by
Jonathan Frakes

Guest Cast: Michelle Forbes, Patti Yasutake,
Kelsey Grammer

119. "The First Duty"
Written by Ronald D. Moore and Naren Shankar;
Directed by Paul Lynch
Guest Cast: Wil Wheaton, Ray Walston,
Robert Duncan McNeill, Ed Lauter,
Jacqueline Brooks, Richard Fancy, Walker Brandt,
Shannon Fill, Richard Rothenberg

120. "Cost of Living"
Written by Peter Allan Fields; Directed by
Winrich Kolbe
Guest Cast: Majel Barrett, Brian Bonsall, Tony Jay,
Carel Struycken, David Oliver, Albie Selznick,
Patrick Cronin, Tracy D'Arcy, George Ede,
Christopher Halsted

121. "The Perfect Mate"
Teleplay by Gary Perconte and Michael Piller; Story
by René Echevarria and Gary Perconte; Directed by
Cliff Bole
Guest Cast: Famke Janssen, Tim O'Connor,
Max Grodenchik, Mickey Cottrell, Michael Snyder,
David Paul Needles, Roger Rignack,
Charles Gunning, April Grace

122. "Imaginary Friend"
Teleplay by Edithe Swenson and Brannon Braga;
Story by Jean Louise Matthias, Ronald Wilkerson
and Richard Fligel; Directed by
Gabrielle Beaumont
Guest Cast: Noley Thornton, Shay Astar,
Jeff Allin, Brian Bonsall, Patti Yasutake,
Sheila Franklin

123. "I, Borg"
Written by René Echevarria; Directed by
Robert Lederman
Guest Cast: Jonathan Del Arco, Whoopi Goldberg

124. "The Next Phase"
Written by Ronald D. Moore; Directed by
David Carson
Guest Cast: Michelle Forbes, Thomas Kopache,
Susanna Thompson, Shelby Leverington,
Brian Cousins, Kenneth Meseroll

125. "The Inner Light"
Teleplay by Morgan Gendel and Peter Allan Fields;
Story by Morgan Gendel; Directed by
Peter Lauritson
Guest Cast: Margot Rose, Richard Riehle,
Scott Jaeck, Jennifer Nash, Patti Yasutake,
Daniel Stewart

126. "Time's Arrow, Part I"
Teleplay by Joe Menosky and Michael Piller; Story
by Joe Menosky; Directed by Les Landau
Guest Cast: Jerry Hardin, Michael Aron,
Barry Kivel, Ken Thorley, Sheldon Peters
Wolfchild, Jack Murdock, Marc Alaimo,
Milt Tarver, Michael Hungerford, Whoopi Goldberg

SEASON SIX (1992-93)

127. "Time's Arrow, Part II"
Teleplay by Jeri Taylor; Story by Joe Menosky;
Directed by Les Landau
Guest Cast: Jerry Hardin, Michael Aron, Barry
Kivel, Ken Thorley, Sheldon Peters Wolfchild,
Jack Murdock, Marc Alaimo, Milt Tarver,
Michael Hungerford, Whoopi Goldberg

128. "Realm of Fear"
Written by Brannon Braga; Directed by Cliff Bole
Guest Cast: Dwight Schultz, Colm Meaney,
Patti Yasutake, Renata Scott, Thomas Belgrey

129. "Man of the People"
Written by Frank Abatemarco; Directed by
Winrich Kolbe

Guest Cast: Chip Lucia, Stephanie Erb,
Susan Rench, Rick Scarry, J.P. Hubbell,
Lucy Boryer, George D. Wallace

130. "Relics"
Written by Ronald D. Moore; Directed by
Alexander Singer
Guest Cast: James Doohan, Lanei Chapman,
Erick Weiss, Stacie Foster, Ernie Mirich

131. "Schisms"
Teleplay by Brannon Braga; Story by Ronald
Wilkerson and Jean Matthias; Directed by
Robert Wiemer
Guest Cast: Lanei Chapman

132. "True Q"
Written by René Echevarria; Directed by
Robert Scherrer
Guest Cast: Olivia D'Abo, John deLancie

133. "Rascals"
Teleplay by Allison Hock; Story by Ward Botsford,
Diana Dru Botsford, and Michael Piller; Directed by
Adam Nimoy
Guest Cast: David Tristan Birkin, Brian Bonsall,
Michael Snyder, Michelle Forbes, Rosalind Chao

134. "A Fistful of Datas"
Teleplay by Robert Hewitt Wolfe and Brannon
Braga; Story by Robert Hewitt Wolfe; Directed by
Patrick Stewart
Guest Cast: Brian Bonsall

135. "The Quality of Life"
Written by Naren Shankar; Directed by
Jonathan Frakes
Guest Cast: Ellen Bry

136. "Chain of Command, Part I"
Teleplay by Ronald D. Moore; Story by
Frank Abatemarco; Directed by Robert Scheerer
Guest Cast: Ronny Cox, David Warner

137. "Chain of Command, Part II"
Written by Frank Abatemarco; Directed by
Les Landau
Guest Cast: Ronny Cox, David Warner

138. "Ship in a Bottle"
Written by René Echevarria; Directed by
Alexander Singer
Guest Cast: Daniel Davis, Dwight Schultz,
Stephanie Beacham

139. "Aquiel"
Teleplay by Brannon Braga and Ronald D. Moore;
Story by Jeri Taylor; Directed by Cliff Bole
Guest Cast: Renee Jones, Reg E. Cathay

140. "Face of the Enemy"
Teleplay by Naren Shankar; Story by René
Echevarria; Directed by Gabrielle Beaumont
Guest Cast: Carolyn Seymour, Scott MacDonald

141. "Tapestry"
Written by Ronald D. Moore; Directed by
Les Landau
Guest Cast: John deLancie, Ned Vaughn,
J. C. Brandy, Suzie Plakson, Clint Carmichael,
Nick Dimitin, Tom Morga

142. "Birthright, Part I"
Written by Brannon Braga; Directed by
Winrich Kolbe
Guest Cast: Siddig El Fadil, James Cromwell

143. "Birthright, Part II"
Written by René Echevarria; Directed by Dan Curry
Guest Cast: Alan Scarfe, Richard Herd,
Christine Rose, Sterling Macer Jr., Jennifer Gatti

144. "Starship Mine"
Written by Morgan Gendel; Directed by Cliff Bole
Guest Cast: David Spielberg, Tim Russ,
Marie Marshall, Patricia Tallman, Tom Nibley,
Glenn Morshower, Alan Altshuld, Tim de Zarn

145. "Lessons"
Written by Ronald Wilkerson and Jean Louise
Matthias; Directed by Robert Weimer
Guest Cast: Wendy Hughes

146. "The Chase"
Teleplay by Joe Menosky; Story by Ronald Moore
and Joe Menosky; Directed by Jonathan Frakes
Guest Cast: Norman Lloyd, Linda Thorson,
John Cothran Jr., Maurice Roeves, Salome Jens

147. "Frame of Mind"
Written by Brannon Braga; Directed by
Jim Conway
Guest Cast: Andrew Prine, Gary Werntz,
David Selburg, Susanna Thompson

148. "Suspicions"
Written by Joe Menosky and Naren Shankar;
Directed by Cliff Bole
Guest Cast: Whoopi Goldberg, Peter Slutsker,
James Horan, Joan Stuart Morris, Tricia O'Neil

149. "Rightful Heir"
Teleplay by Ronald D. Moore; Story by
James E. Brooks; Directed by Winrich Kolbe
Guest Cast: Kevin Conway, Robert O'Reilly

150. "Second Chances"
Teleplay by René Echevarria; Story by
Michael A. Medlock; Directed by LeVar Burton
Guest Cast: Mae Jemison

151. "Timescape"
Written by Brannon Braga; Directed by
Adam Nimoy

152. "Descent, Part I"
Teleplay by Ronald D. Moore; Story by Jeri Taylor;
Directed by Alexander Singer
Guest Cast: Stephen Hawking, Jim Norton,
John Neville

SEASON SEVEN (1993-94)

153. "Descent, Part II"
Written by René Echevarria; Directed by
Alexander Singer
Guest Cast: Stephen Hawking, Jim Norton,
John Neville

154. "Liaisons"
Teleplay by Jeanne Carrigan-Fauci and Lisa Rich;
Story by Roger Eschbacher and Jaq Greenspan;
Directed by Cliff Bole
Guest Cast: Barbara Williams

155. "Interface"
Written by Joe Menosky; Directed by
Robert Wiemer
Guest Cast: Madge Sinclair, Ben Vereen

156. "Gambit, Part I"
Teleplay by Naren Shankar; Story by
Christopher Hatton and Naren Shankar; Directed by
Alexander Singer
Guest Cast: Robin Curtis, Richard Lynch

157. "Gambit, Part II"
Teleplay by Naren Shankar; Story by
Christopher Hatton and Naren Shankar; Directed by
Alexander Singer
Guest Cast: Robin Curtis, Richard Lynch

158. "Phantasms"
Written by Brannon Braga; Directed by
Patrick Stewart

159. "Dark Page"
Written by Hilary J. Bader, Directed by
Les Landau
Guest Cast: Majel Barrett

160. "Attached"
Teleplay by Naren Shankar; Story by
Nicholas Sagan; Directed by Jonathan Frakes

161. "Force of Nature"
Written by Naren Shankar; Directed by
Robert Lederman

162. "Inheritance"
Teleplay by Dan Koeppel and René Echevarria;
Story by Dan Koeppel; Directed by Robert Scheerer

163. "Parallels"
Written by Brannon Braga; Directed by
Robert Wiemer

164. "The Pegasus"
Written by Ronald D. Moore; Directed by LeVar Burton
Guest Cast: Terry O'Quinn

165. "Homeward"
Teleplay by Naren Shankar; Story by
Spike Steingasser; Directed by Alexander Singer
Guest Cast: Paul Sorvino

166. "Sub Rosa"
Teleplay by Brannon Braga; Story by Jeri Taylor;
Directed by Jonathan Frakes

167. "Lower Decks"
Teleplay by René Echevarria; Story by
Ronald Wilkerson and Jean Louise Matthias;
Directed by Gabrielle Beaumont
Guest Cast: Shannon Fill

168. "Thine Own Self"
Teleplay by Ronald D. Moore; Story by
Christopher Hatton; Directed by Winrich Kolbe

169. "Masks"
Written by Joe Menosky; Directed by
Robert Wiemer

170. "Eye of the Beholder"
Teleplay by René Echevarria; Story by
Brannon Braga; Directed by Cliff Bole

171. "Genesis"
Written by Brannon Braga; Directed by
Gates McFadden

172. "Journey's End"
    Written by Ronald D. Moore; Directed by
    Corey Allen
    Guest Cast: Wil Wheaton, Eric Menyuk
173. "Firstborn"
    Teleplay by René Echevarria; Story by
    Mark Kalbfeld; Directed by Jonathan West
    Guest Cast: Brian Bonsall
174. "Bloodlines"
    Written by Nicholas Sagan; Directed by Les Landau
    Guest Cast: Lee Arenberg, Ken Olandt
175. "Emergence"
    Teleplay by Joe Menosky; Story by Brannon Braga;
    Directed by Cliff Bole
176. "Preemptive Strike"
    Teleplay by René Echevarria; Story by
    Naren Shankar; Directed by Patrick Stewart
    Guest Cast: Michelle Forbes
177/178. "All Good Things"
    Special two-hour series finale
    Written by Ronald D. Moore and Brannon Braga;
    Directed by Winrich Kolbe
    Guest Cast: John deLancie

JAMES VAN HISE writes about film, television, and comic book history. He has written numerous books on these subjects, including *Batmania, Horror in the 80s, The Trek Crew Book, Stephen King & Clive Barker: The Illustrated Guide to the Masters of the Macabre*, and *How to Draw Art for Comic Books: Lessons from the Masters*. He is the publisher of *Midnight Graffiti*, in which he has run previously unpublished stories by Stephen King and Harlan Ellison. Van Hise and his wife reside in San Diego along with their horses and various other animals.